LIBERATING YOUR PASSIONATE SOUL

LEVANAH SHELL BDOLAK

Bloomington, IN      Milton Keynes, UK

authorHOUSE®

AuthorHouse™
1663 Liberty Drive, Suite 200
Bloomington, IN 47403
www.authorhouse.com
Phone: 1-800-839-8640

AuthorHouse™ UK Ltd.
500 Avebury Boulevard
Central Milton Keynes, MK9 2BE
www.authorhouse.co.uk
Phone: 08001974150

First published by AuthorHouse 1/9/2007

ISBN: 978-1-4259-7433-6 (sc)

Library of Congress Control Number: 2006909536

Printed in the United States of America
Bloomington, Indiana

This book is printed on acid-free paper.

Cover Image Copyright 2006 Minoo Saboori
www.edencentral.com

DEDICATION

This book is dedicated to my friends, clients and students who have always wanted to do something but could not allow themselves to do it. May courage prevail. May you find the love within you to liberate your passionate soul and live the life you were truly meant to have!

With special thanks to Hiroko Takahashi, Taketoshi Hayashi and Daiki Naganuma for making this book become a reality, and to Nathalie Goldrain and Gabriel Goldrain for their incredible support.

TABLE OF CONTENTS

INTRODUCTION
Investigating Your Passionate Soul

I am a clairvoyant consultant who gives people information to empower themselves. As part of this work, I read auras, the energy field around a person's body. The energy I see is filled with information that enables people to make decisions and understand their own motivations.

A clairvoyant is not a fortuneteller, however, and I don't tell people what to do. Neither do I guarantee that a specific thing will happen in the future, although sometimes I do mention to individuals certain of their strong tendencies to act a particular way. But, I always explain how to change their direction if they want to.

I also train people in skills to relieve stress, change negative or restrictive patterns and develop clairvoyant seeing. In fact, I offer a wide range of global seminars (Clearsight) in self-empowerment techniques—from stress management for CEOs to energy medicine for health-oriented and self-empowerment audiences. Everywhere I go, regardless of race, class or culture, people seem to have the same basic problems. They get out of touch with their passionate soul and buy into what everyone else tells them to do. They often forget to be just who they are and to live as the natural, passionate self in its full glory.

Like everyone else in the world, I view life through my own personal experience. Since I was young, I have always had intuitive experiences. I would know things about people and events, both in the present and the future. I took all of this information for granted, until I got into my twenties and discovered that not everyone was having the same experience. Friends started coming to me for my "experiential counseling" because I could see what really motivated their actions. They would say that I could "see into their souls." So, I tried to show them how to connect with their own soul essence. In time, I met many clairvoyants who had trained to read the aura, and eventually I studied more deeply.

Clairvoyants are both a new and an ancient breed of seer. I soon discovered that clairvoyance is a fascinating combination of superstition and unexacting science, or what some scientists sneer at and call metaphysics. Spiritualists call this realm "beyond the great beyond," and regular folks call it "way out there."

There are clairvoyants who read the bumps on your head, the shape of your jaw and the bone structure of your face to predict your future or your health. There are clairvoyants who can see ancient curses *and* remove them. Some clairvoyants can read your underarms, your palms, your cards and your favorite photos. And others can read your aura, the somewhat invisible life force energy that surrounds your body. Whether or not any of these readings actually tell you the truth or give you life-changing information is entirely up to you to decide.

When I first met other clairvoyants, I quickly discovered that they all had about the same thing to say to me at the same time. For an unexacting science, this clairvoyance certainly seemed mysteriously predictable. For instance, I had a friend who seemed to know almost all the public clairvoyants in town, and when I spent time with her we would run into them one by one. They would pause, look at me, pronounce their one sentence reading and then run off without any thought about what they had just delivered. For one week, every clairvoyant I met told me that I was extremely psychic and destined to be an author. None of these clairvoyants knew more than my first name, but they all said the same thing. It was fascinating and frightening and, of course, I did not know what to make of it.

By the next week, however, I would have somehow shifted my energy, and one of the intuitives would give me some gem about my connection with my mother or the esoteric ability I had to give to the world. And, sure enough, all week long, every clairvoyant I met would mention the same exact piece of information. None of the clairvoyants were connected to any of the others, so I know there was no giant conspiracy in which they would all tell me the same piece of information. I concluded that something in me had triggered their similar pronouncements.

Soon, I became fascinated enough to learn more so that I could understand the different methods of receiving information. I wanted to know how to utilize this knowledge in a specific manner that could actually help people to change, grow and understand themselves. Naturally, the more I learned, the more I found out how much more there was to learn!

WHY I WROTE THIS BOOK

On my journey, I discovered that everything you could want to see about most people is in their aura. Their motivations, past lives, experiences, loves and fears are all like little images stored there. I also discovered that just knowing this information would not necessarily change things for people. So, I studied how to help them shift their energy to release fear and blocks. Over a period of time, I discovered the many different ways we can choose to live out our karma on the dharmic wheel of life. We truly do have the Free Will to make the choice.

Once I had discovered that Free Will is a dominant force in the universe, I began counseling and teaching from a whole new perspective. In

1980, I formed an intuitive center and school with other like-minded people, and we developed a program that would enable others to use their intuitive abilities in practical ways—at home, in business, or just for a better emotional and mental life. We discovered that once you acknowledge your spiritual self, by using certain intuitive skills, you naturally develop to a higher spiritual level as well as become a better human being.

We found that your spiritual life and internal emotional life connect when validating your spiritual nature through the body. We facilitated this validation process by introducing people to the skills of Grounding, Center of the Head and Running Energy—a process that allows your body to feel safe and real by attaching your energy to the planet. Then you will be ready to bring your soul consciousness directly into the body—consciously and wide awake.

Watching people use these skills, the teachers at our center were totally amazed. We saw students change from stuck, fearful and unloved to healthy, happy, loving, courageous and powerful. We saw the total transformation that Christians call Christ consciousness, that Buddhists call Enlightenment or reflection of the inner Buddha nature or that still others might describe as finding the Divine within. We witnessed such incredible transformation in those who practiced these simple skills on a daily basis that we vowed to share this knowledge with as many people as possible. This book is the result of my vow.

WHAT YOU WILL FIND IN THIS BOOK

If you liberate your passionate nature and define your path in life, you can take charge of your own destiny. Sometimes people feel that it is wrong to follow your passionate nature. After all, Buddha said that desire is the cause of all pain and suffering in life. Following your true passionate nature, however, is not necessarily satisfying your desires. Following your true passionate nature is finding what you do best, where your talents and abilities lie, what you really came here to do in this life and what makes you feel good. Your passionate nature is the agenda of your body personality, the part of you that expresses your inner self to the outer world. Expressing your passionate soul is doing what comes naturally.

In this book, I discuss the nature of the passionate soul and how you can understand that powerful part of yourself. Presented in the appendix are exercises, guided meditations and energy devices for connecting with your true inner passionate nature. It is up to you to be the prime mover in your life. Connecting with your true inner nature will take you to your success, your true love and the inner peace of your being. Moreover, the stories and guidance in these chapters can help you achieve the best possible health for your body, which will enable you to do what you've chosen to do.

What do you want to do with the new energy you discover? It has been my belief that how much energy you have is not as important as how you use it. For example, you may have skills that enable you to have a wonderful, beautiful life, but life is not just the experience of having everything go well. It is also the ability to use your good fortune to improve the world around you. To take your skills and give unselfishly of yourself to others and the planet is to truly be the God Force Within.

Once you have merged your essence with the higher spiritual forces in the universe—with which you consciously move to join your higher, finer nature—you become a "connected" human being. You can now move from being a bystander in the play of life to an action-oriented, powerfully motivated, positively aligned individual.

When we align our higher spiritual nature with our passionate soul, we are always on-line. We become more conscious with every passing moment. This awareness enables us to focus our life energies to create a better world. We are able to have visions of our dreams for our children and the generations to come. To this end, we become better parents, friends, workers, lovers and visionaries. We become the people we have always dreamed about. We have the ability to become our own heroes and heroines, to shift the consciousness of the entire world, making it a better, happier, more fulfilling place for everyone.

This may seem a dauntless task that would take centuries and beyond, but in the spiritual world, where there is no time or space, shifting energy is instantaneous. And, for courageous passionate souls, shifting the quality of the world around us is entirely within our own making. We become one with the Buddha, the Christ, the God or Goddess, the Light or the Essence of Love, transforming all whom we meet and all that we do.

Chapter 1
Where Is Your Passionate Soul?

Are you happy with your life? We all know that happiness is usually transitory. In the course of a few minutes, you can be alternately flooded with emotions that run the gamut of joy and delight to sadness and desolation. So let me ask this in another way. Are you in touch with the passion in your life?

Do you get up in the morning happy with yourself, happy to share your life with your spouse or family, eager to go to work and to feel totally involved with your actions? Or are you bored, feeling stuck in a lackluster job, at odds with your family, uncomfortable with accomplishments or lack of them and generally uninterested in your own existence? Is your passionate nature alive, or is it hidden or worse yet, dead?

For some people, experiencing their passionate self means watching an action film for the evening. Are you living vicariously through TV, movies, magazines and newspapers? Do you celebrate and enjoy your sexuality and sensuality or are they unfulfilled, ignored, or swept under the rug? If more than 30 percent of your life is unfulfilled, then you have somehow allowed the passionate soul of your own true nature to be lost to your waking self.

What is the passionate soul?

We all have a soul. It expresses itself through what excites you about life. Your soul nature is your energetic essence or what you came here to do. Your mind is the willpower that spins the wheel of passion. Now you might not be religious, or might not even believe in the soul, but you may have come to realize that a person impassioned is a person with a zest for a life, a person with pizzazz. Children all have this zest for life. They always have an incredible ability to be in the moment and to enjoy the thrill of living and learning. The only time I have seen children without this passionate flame is when they are starving or abused—physically or emotionally.

Somewhere, though, between the end of childhood and the beginning of adulthood, this wonderful passion for living is usually lost. So many adults express dullness, a loss of energy and excitement mirrored by the glazed-over look in their eyes that says, "I am not really here. I'm thinking about the work I must do, the errands I must accomplish and the vacation I wish I could take. I am escaping—running away from my feelings, from the feelings of my body and from all the responsibilities I seem to be accountable for."

Many people have this lack of responsiveness constantly unless prodded with super excitement in the form of violence, sex or food. As a result, they overeat, obsess with sex or violence and fear checking in with their true inner feelings.

But the passionate soul is not dead. You do not have to overeat to feel good. You do not have to fantasize or obsess to enjoy sex. You do not have to watch violent TV horror movies to feel alive! The passionate soul within every person is always there just waiting for permission to be liberated into action. Being passionate is the right of every human being.

ARE YOU IN TOUCH WITH YOUR PASSIONATE SOUL?

One day, a middle-aged, fairly good-looking woman walked into my office. She was kind of nervous, but that is not unusual. Because I am a clairvoyant reader, people come to me to find out the things they already know but do not know they know. So they sweat in fear of the truths they will be told and often fidget and jump nervously.

I smiled at the woman, trying to make her feel relaxed as she sat herself in a comfortable chair across from me. Then I closed my eyes to look at her aura and asked what she wanted to know.

"I'm getting a divorce," she said with a sad tone in her voice. "Am I doing the right thing?"

Well, I am a clairvoyant, but I am not mommy to my clients. I do not *tell* them what to do; I just give them information. I asked for her husband's first name and his physical description and then held his energy next to hers to see what they did together. It looked like they did *nothing* together. These two persons had been married for twenty years, and there was no longer any passion for them. Specifically, his energy was not sparked by his wife; he looked like he wanted to walk away, sit in front of the TV, watch a game and stuff his face with "fat food." She, on the other hand, just walked away—and she was walking toward another man.

"You have become involved with someone else," I found myself saying, "someone who makes you feel young and alive and passionate, yes?"

"Yes," she admitted.

It was hard for me to keep reading her from a clairvoyant place. First, I had to get into a neutral, nonjudgmental state and stay there. Personally, I believe that someone is married until divorced. My father had been a promiscuous man, which hurt my mother immensely. I believe in the purity of the bonds of marriage and in not interrupting those vows until they are formally broken. It is not, however, my place to judge another's actions. A clairvoyant reads. God judges.

The woman proceeded to tell me how she had struggled for years to rejuvenate her marriage, but nothing had worked. Having given up, she was living a boring existence relegated to the land of sexual limbo. One day, though, she had accidentally met a man to whom she was attracted. She had never experienced anything like this before, neither in the beginning of her marriage nor even with her first teenage love.

Suddenly, she had discovered lust and love and, most of all, a passion for life. On some level, she still deeply loved her husband, but the joy and the spark had been all but wiped out of the marriage. Only their old patterns and the acceptance of a milk-toast life together remained. She wanted more. She had always wanted more, and now in some miraculous manner she had found it. Her life had become a live romance novel, and she was willing to risk everything to run with her new feelings. Perhaps it would last a week—or maybe the rest of her lifetime. Most of all, the passion did exist right now—and she wanted it badly.

And so her question was, "Am I doing the right thing in getting this divorce?"

So I looked at the woman with the new man in her life. Yes, he was a live wire, joyous and full of action. More important, there was something about him that gave her the permission to act out her passionate nature. Suddenly, she was doing what she *wanted* to do. Her situation was not so much about a sexual affair as about deciding what type of life she really wanted. She was feeling her passionate nature for waking up every morning with a zest for living, experiencing every moment that she could and truly expressing her feelings.

I also explained that she could turn on her own passionate nature. True, her children were grown and she could leave her husband behind, going off into the sunset with a new lover. But she didn't need to depend on anyone outside of herself to make her feel alive. Whether this relationship lasted or not, she would always be able to access her special nature of aliveness, her passion for life. Therefore, it wasn't really the new relationship or the hot sex or the change of partner that sparked her as much as the permission she was feeling to go with her inner passion. And this permission is something one can give to oneself.

DO YOU GIVE PERMISSION TO YOUR PASSIONATE SELF?

I am not sure if the loss of the passionate soul is a modern-century issue or a deeper condition of the human race. I do believe, however, that everyone must address this issue to have a life worth living. If you truly want to be alive every moment, you will need to acknowledge and act out of your passionate self. Otherwise, you are lost.

The religious people will say you are lost to God. The spiritual people will say you are lost to your Higher Self. Your boss will say you are lost or out of touch with your work. Your spouse will say that your marriage has lost its zest. Your children will see that you have lost the ability to have fun. And if you are just moving through the motions, there is nothing much left that will excite you. The following story illustrates what I mean.

I once had a business client in Tokyo. An affable young man in his early thirties, he was on his way up the career ladder. He knew how to position himself for the most exciting jobs, but whenever he spoke of the ladies in his life, his voice would lower into a nervous stutter. He was a well-dressed, handsome young man with good manners, but he could never find a woman who fit him. One day, he took me sightseeing around the temples, shrines and hot spots of Tokyo. At the end of the day, I did the truly American act of hugging him goodbye. This is when I noticed something about him that was troubling.

Japanese people, as a rule, do not hug or kiss in public. They do not even touch in public. This young man, however, had lived in America. When we hugged (at his suggestion), he visibly jumped, as if to psychically run away, and then stuttered his goodbyes. The next time I saw him, I got him to talk about his episodes with women. It soon became obvious that he could not connect with his passion for a woman because he was afraid of their power. Whenever he could not connect with his internal passion or deal with his inner feelings, he would stammer and bumble. Suddenly, this articulate businessman would have too much information coming out too quickly, to avoid saying what he was really feeling inside. Because he did not see himself as being strong, he had no permission to act out of his passions and to express his strong masculine nature. Slowly, I began to introduce him to the intuitive skills for getting in touch with one's own needs and passions and for allowing permission to express them to others.

ARE YOU CONTROLLED BY OTHERS' PASSIONS?

The nature of a clairvoyant psychic is to be sensitive. Sometimes, however, we are thought of as oversensitive. For example, I can be in a room with someone who is hungry and I will be hungry. But if the person leaves the room, I will stop being hungry. I can feel a person's pain or their fear or love. It took me a few years to learn that this was not *my* fear or pain or love. I had to learn to make a clear separation so I could understand where these extra emotions were coming from. The following story describes a situation in which I learned more about how to know my own mind.

Years ago, I used to perm my hair to give it body. I have always had thin, baby fine hair. Where I inherited it from, I've never known. Many of the people in my family have thick, wavy or curly hair and olive-colored skin, while I somehow came out of the womb with pinkish skin, blue eyes and limp blondish brown hair that holds a curl only if sprayed with buckets of superhold spray. So I permed my hair to give it body and, to my way of thinking, everything was great. But on exceptionally rainy days my hair would frizz into a ball of fuzz as if I had stuck my finger in an electrical socket. At that time, I was an insecure widow and going out with a very opinionated ex-Hollywood book agent. He was forever trying to remake me into his idea of the perfect Hollywood speaker.

"You have to get your hair fixed so that it is neater, so that you can look slick when you get on the *Oprah* show," he would repeat endlessly.

I had no offers for the *Oprah* show and was happy the way I was, but one day his prickly nudgings prompted me to ask everyone around what they did to "fix up their hair." With that, people suggested en masse that I go to Christophe's salon in Beverly Hills. In Los Angeles, I have learned, if you ask for the best lawyer or the best makeup artist or the best hairdresser, the outpouring of responses to your request will all point to the same solution, as if the answer were being orchestrated somewhere by an all-knowing oracle. Perhaps it reflects the clone-like nature of the Hollywood crew that makes up this small, tightly knit community. Or, maybe it suggests the gang-like nature of a big city "in" crowd. But once this happens, I (like everyone else, of course) go to the recommended specialist.

I made an appointment to see Christophe, wondering if he was indeed the hairdresser for me. People were saying things like, "He cut the President's hair, you know!" I had no idea what he would do to me, but I did know I was tired of being told my frizzy hair was too unkempt, that I did not make the grade and that I looked "not right." I also was beginning to spend the better part of an hour every morning trying to look good by setting and spraying my hair. Having been a naturalist the better part of my life, I did not take to all the gooey gels that made me feel like a 1950s mannequin.

After a six-week wait for an appointment, finally I graced the door of Christophe's establishment with my eager, albeit naive, head. Like I would expect in any good salon, an attendant handed me a cute but utilitarian robe and placed me in a swivel chair. Christophe finally appeared, introduced himself and immediately began fondling my hair as if he had known me all my adult life. His comments were profuse and made me want to disappear down some rabbit hole, if there had been one handy.

"It is too dry! Too many cut and brittle ends. You have been perming this a long time, no?"

"Yes," I replied. "About twelve years."

"Twelve years!" he repeated as if I had uttered some terrible oath. "This is no good. Your hair is fried! You must, you must stop this immediately," he insisted with the authority assumed only by a seasoned hairdresser.

I began to go into my childish mode, arguing with him and protesting that my hair had absolutely no body and would fall limply flat. He quickly overrode my fears, insisting that when *he* was through, my hair would have sheen and body instead of looking like a dried-out cat someone had stuck into an electrical socket.

"You must not do such gauche things to your hair! You must respect and treat it well," he insisted, as if I had perpetrated the most unacceptable behavior. Then he walked around me once, stroked my hair and declared, "Short . . . and pushed back to show off your face." However, I strangely found myself uttering words about my boyfriend's needs.

"But, he wants me to have long hair," I whined. I could not believe I was actually saying this to Christophe. I felt like I was in high school trying to be one of the "in" crowd. But I could just about hear my boyfriend's voice inside my head pressing me to argue for what he wanted. Meanwhile, my inside self was cringing at the words coming out. Again I fretted, "But my boyfriend. . .," when Christophe capably cut me off.

"It's not what he wants, but what looks good on you. You do not have the face for long hair. It will not look good. It will hang on you. You must go with what your looks give you, and that is short hair. It is *your* hair—not your boyfriend's."

Even though I knew better, I had somehow let myself try to act out my boyfriend's passions. I knew what I had said was not only wrong for me, but also ridiculous. I was not some teenager who needed to be accepted.

And, even though as a somewhat insecure widow, I was knowledgeable enough to know my own mind and my own head of hair. I sat there stunned by my lack of ownership over my body.

Christophe finished his artistry after twenty minutes (which probably would have taken only half the time if I hadn't foolishly argued with him the whole while) and quickly handed me over to his salon crew. They washed and cut me and, voila, within three weeks, as my hair grew out of the perm, I had a new and healthy hairstyle. I got compliments for months to come. My hair looked really good, but the real lesson in the experience was to listen to the voice inside of me, to follow my own needs. For years, I had counseled others about how not to be dominated by their lovers and coworkers and then had started to do that very thing.

ACTING OUT YOUR TRUE EMOTIONS

It is not unusual for people to be unaware of their feelings, not able to tell the difference between their own emotions and the other guy's. They often strive to please their friends and relatives, doing what everyone else wants and sometimes making the wrong decisions. Over the years, clairvoyants have developed skills to help people easily respond to their own passions instead of always playing someone else's hand in the game of life.

Several years ago, I found a friend of mine ringing the bell at my front door. At seven o'clock at night in my neighborhood, this is unthinkable! As a matter of fact, at any time of day or night, it is rare to see another living soul on my front porch. I've had only three unannounced visitors ever. Even my neighbor at the bottom of the road calls before coming over!

I live in the rustic countryside just outside of Los Angeles where there are no streetlights or sidewalks. One sees only winding canyon roads, cute wild rabbits, owls that hunt the cute rabbits and coyote packs that gather nightly to howl at their cornered prey. Most likely they are hot after a cute little rabbit—or some neighbor's pet that didn't make it into the house in time for the evening news. Once the sun goes down and the sky is awash with stars, and even though I am but a short drive to a modern mall, it seems as if I am ferreted away in the wild expanse of the western frontier.

It helps, of course, that my house is at the end of the road, at a little known entrance to a state park. Basically, I am surrounded on three sides by not much more than scrub brush and giant boulders. So, when a person shows up, especially at night, I usually don't even recognize my own doorbell. To help me, my husband hung up an ethnic-type bell with a manual clapper, which makes a much larger reverberating noise. Even when this bell rings, however, I am apt to believe it is just the Santa Ana winds knocking about because who in the world could possibly be at my front door?

Therefore, I was totally surprised when I heard the bell and discovered one of my lady friends in tears on the front doorstep. This was a strong-woman type who owned her own business and had a successful husband and two young children as well. She always seemed together and on top of things, even when everyone else was floundering in the normal chaos we call mere living. Thus, I was doubly surprised to see her in such a disheveled state. Ushering her into my tiny country-style living room, I offered a soothing tea and immediately became her listening post. She was red-eyed and blubbering, alternately blowing her nose and spewing copious tears. It took awhile for her to become calm enough so I could understand what she was saying. It went something like this: "I always promised myself that I would never be like my mother. And now, I'm just like her."

At first, I could not quite grasp what she was talking about. To my mind, we are all like our mothers, although in our younger years we tend to deny this idea. Finally, she was composed enough to tell me the whole story of how her mother used to yell at her, repeating certain key phrases over and over. My friend had promised that she would always listen to her own children and not repeat such tired phrases ad nauseam.

"What kind of phrases?" I asked.

"My mother would say things like, 'What will you do when I die and am no longer here to help you?' or, 'You have no common sense!'" she answered.

She felt that her mother was always putting her down, invalidating her ability by making her seem not good enough. So she had promised to never, yes *never,* do that to *her* child. And yet, just this afternoon when her daughter had done something totally aggravating, out of her own mouth had come one of her mother's favorite phrases. It had just popped out unbidden, unthought-of, but nonetheless it had been spoken. And worse, she felt she had uttered the words harshly.

"I was in a hurry and had a client waiting. I just lost it, I guess," she said as if to apologize. She continued to cry and beat herself up emotionally, going on and on with, "But how could I have done that? It's like I had no control!"

I sat my friend down and calmly tried to explain that humans are products of extensive habituation and programming. In fact, we stay "babies" the longest of any animal. By comparison, other animals become adults quite quickly, in the course of a few months to a year or two. However, humans are tied to their families well beyond their eighteen or so formative years. It's no wonder most grownups are constantly trying to undo the patterns and emotional behaviors they have received from their loving parents.

I had seen many parents experiencing the same dichotomy that my friend was going through. "Beating yourself up won't change your behavior," I explained. In between cups of tea, I illustrated how patterns and programs move us away from expressing our passions, and how clairvoyants have developed some simple skills for releasing old patterns and programs. I taught her two releasing techniques, gave her a giant hug and a big box of tissues and sent her home much relieved.

When demonstrating how to release old programs, I first asked if she could still hear her mother yelling those infamous, repetitive phrases. "Yes, I can hear her in my head as if she were here right now."

"This is very common," I replied. "Emotional imprints can stick with us for years and later pop out as our own belief."

At first, children adore their parents and put them on a pedestal, but when the children become teenagers, they often balk at parental authority. Actually, they are just trying to make their own individual way and at this age typically turn to peers for support. If certain behavior patterns are being forced upon the children, however, they may later react without knowing why. For example, in their twenties, they may have trouble with a boss or an authority symbol who reminds them of their parents. By their thirties, they are probably in the parental role too and perhaps doing exactly what they have been resenting. My parents called this process growing up. But as a clairvoyant consultant, I call it being stuck in your parents' programming or repeating their emotional behavioral patterns. And when you do this, you lose touch with your own emotions and your own passionate self.

Once you can recognize hearing your mother or father "talking" in your head, or realize you are doing what they did (even though you do not really agree with it), then you can learn to permanently release their energy and finally "grow up." You can learn to be totally in touch with your own emotional nature, be your "true" self.

Since I have learned to release the patterning of my mother, for example, I look back and love her more than ever without fearing I might take on the parts of her behavior I did not like. I can now be my own person and act out of my own passionate nature. Many people do not do this growing up until well into their sixties. Ideally, we should all do this in our early twenties so we can express more love to our parents as well as learn to live our own lives.

Chapter 2
Doing What You Love To Do

Today, many people appear to be out of touch with their occupations. Perhaps they are bored, uninterested, uninspired and working only for the money. If so, they have lost their passion for what they are doing. Often, we have to wonder if they ever had any passion for it in the first place. What does it take to follow your passionate soul at work? After all, your work is what you do the most of in life.

One day, a young woman in her early thirties called for a general clairvoyant reading. I saw her energy turn a beautiful turquoise blue that seemed to stretch out from her. I said, "You are going to have some money coming in."

"Everyone tells me this," she agreed.

"Everyone?" I asked.

It seems that she had called just about every clairvoyant in town, and they all said that soon she would make a lot of money. "But it hasn't come true," she added wistfully.

I asked what she was doing to help make it happen. "Nothing. I'm just sitting in bed and eating pizza," was her genuine reply.

I tried to explain the basic principles of how humans create reality. "When people tell you something about what is coming in the future, they are not making it happen for you. You need to do it for yourself. You cannot just sit there in bed. You have to go into the world and be a part of the action." I then suggested that she take the abundance seminar I was teaching.

A month later, she took the seminar, but I did not see or hear from her until a year later when she called for another phone reading. "How is your money doing?" I asked.

"Just great. Couldn't be better." She had opened her own business, was totally impassioned and was wildly making money. "But now," she said yearningly, "I want to create a relationship."

This lady exemplifies the qualities that make a person successful. If you follow your passion in life, do what excites you and do it well, doors are bound to keep opening.

WHY SO MUCH FEAR, SO MANY EXCUSES?

Not everyone has yet had the experience I've just described, however, nor can they figure out why not. I watched the head of Crown Books being interviewed on CNN. Sadly, he could not understand why some of his employees were not as excited as he was about building the company. If you have read business self-help books over the last eight or ten years, you will know that top CEOs and entrepreneurs are all passionate creatures. They are obsessed (politely called "focused") on getting to their goal because what they do interests and inspires them. Filled with passion, they typically do their work well and are successful.

Nevertheless, I have counseled many CEOs, business managers and executives in a mid-life crisis, which often involves being laid off, bought off or asked to leave a downsizing company. These problems are often attributed to changes in the global economy brought about by the U.S. recession of the early 1990s, the bursting bubble in Japan in the late '80s and early '90s and subsequent economic woes in Pacific Rim countries as they tried to fit ineffective strategies into a world system. More recently, the world has had to contend with the financial and political repercussions of 9/11, a climate of war and terrorism and the outsourcing of many jobs from the United States to other countries.

As people lose middle-management jobs, they first go into terror, then fear and then long-lasting depression. They may come from losing a good middle-class income with little hope of finding a similar long-range situation, a frightening prospect for both breadwinners and their families. When companies trim away what they see as unnecessary or unaffordable, dismissed middle-management workers can no longer command the salaries they are used to. With the increase in company outsourcing, familiar job avenues virtually dry up, and workers must look for alternatives. They have to be open to new ways of being a salaried person, or they need to become entrepreneurs in countries where money is scarce and raising investment funding is difficult, if not close to impossible. Suddenly, they are forced to think in totally different ways that often go even beyond what we used to call creative financing.

I discovered, however, that when an economy goes through hard times and the jobless have to shift to other careers and ways of earning a living, many people—not all, but many—find something they are more impassioned about. It is almost as if an invisible force in the universe pushes them further along their path into a type of work for which they have more energy or interest. Some of my clients found new careers in the middle of a financial downturn and later were actually happier because of it, strange as that might seem. When the financial climate finally recovered, they had survived harrowing experiences by harnessing new resources of inner strength and integrity. Further, a large percentage realized that their new work was closer to their innate passionate nature. Sometimes when you are in the wrong place, the powers that be give you a push toward a better place.

I travel extensively and everywhere I see similarities among all people. At first, I thought a lot of people were unhappy at work because the industrial revolution has forced those in developing countries to go from brawn to brains, from agrarian farming or animal husbandry to pushing office paper. Well, maybe the women in Tokyo will admit to this if you press them, but the men, having a higher and thus more specific job status, seem to take satisfaction that they are "salaried men" who work in offices. Although people have claimed even more specific titles in the United States since the globalization of our economy, we too have a large variety of office workers in self-employed, retail and service jobs. In addition, a host of service workers exist mainly to service (cloth, feed, design for, sell to) the office people.

This, of course, is an oversimplified perception. But I discovered that even among agrarian people, some are passionate about who they are and what they do and others are bored, uninterested and disenchanted with their work. You may think that by human nature, not all people will be in love with their work. Yes, to a degree this is true. But people take a particular job in a particular profession for a reason.

So, I now ask my clients *why* they are bored, uninterested or downright unhappy with their method of earning a living. The answer may be found in how each day is spent. For example, if you were to look at how you conduct each 24-hour day, you would probably account for the time as follows: eight to twelve hours working, five to eight hours sleeping, one to two hours commuting, one to two hours consuming sustenance and any other time (depending on how much you sleep) in relaxation or entertainment, which is often a nonparticipatory two to three hours of watching TV. On the basis of what you do most, shouldn't your work be the most interesting and engaging action in your life?

DO YOU ACT ON YOUR FEELINGS?

Following your passionate soul is learning to take small but significant risks. It is allowing yourself to *feel* and then *act* on your feelings. It can be scary, no doubt about it. And it sometimes takes practice. But it is infinitely more rewarding than sitting back and watching the people on the tube live your life for you!

Let me give an example of creating true passion by taking a risk at work. I had a client in Los Angeles who had a medium-size construction company of almost one hundred employees. He really enjoyed building houses, but he absolutely hated being in charge of a lot of employees and taking care of everyone like a Big Daddy. After much internal struggle, he finally let go of most of his employees and downsized his company's goals. He made less money, but he really enjoyed his work and went home every night feeling happy. He no longer felt so responsible and could feel content interacting with his small staff. His true passion was in being on the job site instead of being an administrator. For him, downsizing was the best way to true happiness in life.

If you have an active lifestyle, it is easier to follow your passion. This means you are making decisions and choosing what you do. A passive lifestyle consists of sitting on the couch watching more than two hours of TV a day, going to movies or reading books to escape or finding your daily dose of excitement from things outside yourself. When you feel that outside things move you around so that you are not really in charge, you are not in touch with your own passionate power.

To follow an active lifestyle, you need to develop active thought patterns. You might say to yourself things like: "I can change it." "Let's see what I am going to do now." "I can make temporary decisions and if they do not work, I can revise them as I go." "Something inside of me was in conflict or needed to grow, so it created this situation. I now need to understand it and change it."

Passive thought patterns go like this: "Why does this happen to me?" "I wish I could have the money that Bill Gates has." "So and so gets all of the beautiful women," or "all of the handsome men." "That's just the way it is." "You can't fight City Hall." Thoughts of being a victim or not ever able to succeed imply that something outside of you can doom you. This thing might be an aberration, a bad economy, politics, your astrological forecast, a belief system or even believing that the whim of God is choosing for you. But when nothing is stronger than the power within yourself, you can change your life. It may be difficult to quickly change the outside world, but you can easily and quickly change yourself.

If something is not working, it usually means that an aspect of *you* is not in alignment with your goal. Because life is a learning process, this does not mean you should feel guilty or blame yourself. And, when something does not work, you can change it. When learning to walk, for example, children do not experience guilt or blame when they fall down. They just try again until it works. Isn't it befuddling how often adults would rather just sit down, blame themselves and experience old guilt rather than look for a different mode of action? Remember, action follows thought. So find something to do. If nothing seems to work, then reexamine your wants, your needs and how you are doing things.

The woman in the following story reexamined her situation in my Clearsight career program in Tokyo. She wanted to preserve her soul's passion. A beautiful young woman, she loved her work in the computer field and was very good at this. However, she felt that her employer wanted her to work eighteen hours a day. Being young and wanting a social life, she found herself quitting one day in exasperation. She never found another full-time job that suited her, so she took on a wide variety of part-time jobs. She tutored students and performed for parties and children's plays, among other things. But she really wanted to move back to a regular job because just organizing all the small jobs had become quite complex. When I spoke with her, she had three or four very creative jobs yet could not choose which should become her next full-time job.

After much soul searching, she finally realized that she truly loved and enjoyed computer work. Even though computer firms are known for "working you to death," she knew she could find a company that expected no more than normal working hours. Having good skills, she could pick and choose the right kind of job to fit her social lifestyle. She would have to choose carefully and not take a job out of economic fear. She also needed to know exactly the type of job, hours and the kind of company she wanted to work for. And, that is exactly what she chose to do.

WHAT IS YOUR AWAKE QUOTIENT?

Why is this lack of passion in work so prevalent? Are you happy with your work? Is your work a job or a career? A job is something you do for money and to survive, but a career is something you have so much passion for that you will do it whether you get paid or not. If you are in a survival-based job and could move to a higher paying position doing something entirely different, and equally without special meaning to you, you would switch jobs in a nanosecond. But a career is an obsession, a true love and a powerful entity that carries you along so that you wake up each day and cannot wait to get to work—regardless of the compensation.

Are you driven by your true passion or are you just *putting in your time* until you get your pension or can make the rent or mortgage? Are you awake and alive when you are working? Or, are your eyes glazing over, and is the creative part of your brain going to sleep on the job? If the latter is true, you are selling yourself short. You are throwing away your most productive hours, your deepest feelings and your true desires to fit into someone else's reality. This leads you to nowhere but boredom and a stuff-your-face mentality in front of the TV. Or, you may numb yourself with drink at your favorite bar.

Do you know where you stand with your occupation? If you are a job person, ask if something else in your life is filling in for the passion missing in your work. Do you have a sideline hobby, a second career, an out-of-sight love life or a secretive spy job for the government?

Are you open to your passions in another way, on another road? Or, have you locked all the doors and trapped yourself in one room? Are you the well-behaved little trudger who goes to work, comes home and goes back to work the next day? If I mention passion in life, do you stand up to be counted, or do you sigh with yearning or regret?

Some friends in San Francisco were running a job placement agency that helped people find their true occupations after they had lost their work. This was in the late 1980s when many people were being downsized or pensioned off from ailing companies at a fairly young age. One day, a wealthy doctor came to my friends for help. He had everything a person could want, or so they thought. He was blessed with good looks, a lucrative and prestigious practice, a wonderful family and a home life rich in both possessions and relationships. But he was not happy being a doctor. Of course, my friends couldn't understand why he wanted a new occupation, but to help him they put him through their typical career analysis. The doctor took tests, was interviewed while being videotaped and answered a lot of questions.

"What happened to that fellow?" I asked one day.

"He's running a catfish farm on the East Coast," they answered. "According to his tests, he needed to be in charge and have a sense of accomplishment."

After they had put all of the factors together, they suggested the catfish endeavor. At that time, catfish farming was just opening up as a viable business. I remember well the look on my friend's face when he described the doctor's reaction to their solution. "His eyes lit up and suddenly he was a totally different person. Something incredibly alive came awake within him, and you could just see it in his eyes."

My friend was convinced that the doctor would thank them but likely pooh-pooh the idea of beginning again in a different state at the other end of the continent. He was totally surprised when he realized that this business idea began to excite the doctor. The man's eyes unmistakably showed that this was the right answer for him. When something impassions you, it is obvious to you and everyone else, too. It is your life, your karma and your passion, which carries you through the ups and downs, the difficulties and fears, and pushes you into total enjoyment of life.

I couldn't resist asking my friend if he had ever seen this kind of passion in the eyes of his other clients—or even in the eyes of the people he worked with. "Very rarely," he answered. "Very, very rarely."

INCREASING YOUR ABILITY TO SHIFT

The story of the doctor led me to think deeply about being impassioned with what one does in life. Isn't that what life is all about—enjoying what you do and thus doing it well? We can all relate to the resignation or boredom that sets in if we get stuck in the mundane routines of everyday existence. Brushing your teeth, driving to work on the freeway or taking the subway to the same destination every day will not have the same excitement quotient as doing something entirely new.

To children, however, each experience is new and changeable. They are open to wonderment and joy in every situation. In contrast to adults, they won't "accept" boring routines, literally killing themselves a little at a time. Therefore, there must be a way for adults also to preserve this totally alive sense of wonderment, even in the most boring of moments.

Is it so difficult to create the wonderful feeling that makes life worth living? I do not think so, or I would not bother showing my clients simple skills for taking charge of their life choices and inner feelings. Attitude, focus, personal choice and self-direction—these all come into play here. However, if you see the outside world as being stronger than your own choices, you will have no freedom to create. If you believe you can take charge of your attitudes while focusing on the goals you choose, then you indeed do have the ability to make your life (and your career, your love life and your family) a fulfilling and passionate experience.

We all have the ability to shift ourselves into new dimensions of thought and, therefore, action. Often we do not do this and become stuck in fixed modes of behavior. To put it simply: What we know we have might not be what we want, but it is safer than what we do not know! So how do we get beyond this stuck place?

Most people go beyond their stuck places only if they have to. They wait until a mid-life crisis, a work lay-off, or a company bankruptcy, or some similar crisis that seems to be spurred from the outside. Only when pushed against a wall do they change begrudgingly. I find it interesting that the Chinese word for "crisis" can also mean "opportunity." If you can face the fact that your life is moving in the direction of an impending change, then you can make that change flow much more easily than waiting for a crisis.

Releasing illness in your body

Often when people get stuck and lose passion, they also get sick. Healers sometimes say that people who get sick lose spirit, get bored with life or give up trying to change their condition. Perhaps it is that they have been doing something they truly do not want to do.

It seems that when you get out of touch with your essential passionate nature you lose your zest for life. When you lose your zest for life, your life force lessens. It gets deadened and diminished, which makes it is easy for illness to grab hold. By getting in touch with your true loving nature and your true agenda in life, you can release the essential cause of your illness and prevent and cure physical ailments.

Doctors have long known that attitude can affect physical ailments. Pioneering cancer specialists such as Dr. Carl Simonton have shown that feelings, beliefs and attitudes are often a major factor in the onset of disease symptoms. When these charged energy patterns are released, energy blocks expressed as pain and disease begin to shift and change.

Stress release and meditation skills can put you in touch with your ever-present ability to be energetically awake in the moment, so can your attitude. Intuitive techniques can also help you accomplish this. Some are practical measures that businesspeople use every day but do not always apply to their own lives. If you are stuck or facing great changes, you can give yourself permission to change and use the techniques presented in this book. You can choose to be in charge rather than waiting for it all to happen to you. When you choose to change, find new avenues for employment *and* do what truly impassions you, then you are the winner in life.

Chapter 3
Checking in With Yourself

Take the time to ask yourself what you are passionate about and what you are not passionate about. Are you in touch with what is really happening in your life? Are you passionate about the things you dislike? The things you love?

So often we don't check in with ourselves until something goes wrong. I have a lot of clients who come *only* when they are in hot water. People suddenly need a clairvoyant spiritual counselor when family business is in bankruptcy, a lifelong job is lost, close relatives are terminally ill or a teenage child is so unruly that parents are afraid to go home for fear of being beaten up. When these life difficulties happen, it's time to admit that the problem is so big that help from an outside source is needed. But what goes on in the time between the first throws of a problem and the ensuing crisis of disaster, when a person finally acknowledges the need for help?

Recently, I went to a party where some of my clients were present. I almost did not recognize them. They were happily enjoying themselves, appearing relaxed within their personalities and their bodies. How different this was from when they come to see me, usually when they are totally stressed—physically, emotionally and mentally.

Why do people wait to seek help until they are at their worst? Frequently, our cultural and moral values restrict us from taking action. I grew up in a European-style household that was culturally traditional. If you had a problem you simply suffered in silence. It was not acceptable to speak to anyone about your personal emotions. You certainly did not go outside the family to get help. There was no such thing as going to a therapist or psychologist. This was your burden in life, and it was all yours to deal with in the confines of your own private world.

CAN YOU ASK FOR HELP?

Many people have this kind of lifestyle restriction, which I call "lack of permission." If you cannot ask for help, you will usually also try to hide the problem even from yourself! Supposedly, if you do not admit that something is not working, then you don't have to deal with it. However, eventually the problem causes everything else in your life to come to a standstill—and then you *really* have to deal with it.

When you bury your problem, it causes you to feel a little less loving of yourself.

Years ago, I had a friend who was a fairly well-known rock musician. He lived with his girlfriend, but they didn't get along very well. Over a period of about five months, even though he was making a lot of money, he managed to spend or lose it and couldn't afford to keep up their apartment. Eventually, they had to sell everything and move. His girlfriend went to a cousin's home, and he started living in his car. I saw him one day at the local café and asked how he was doing. He gleefully stated that financially he was a mess. He had lots of bookings but no money, and he was basically living on the street.

"You don't look unhappy," I remember telling him.

"Oh, I'm doing well," he replied. "I have just about lost everything I own so my girlfriend no longer wants to live with me. I'll move to Los Angeles and get a little apartment by the beach and be happy now."

"Your girlfriend will not go with you?"

"Oh, thank God, no. Now that I have lost everything, she would be uncomfortable."

I looked at him carefully. Obviously, he had not been able to verbally announce the end of the relationship. So, he had "engineered" apparent losses and rid himself of his girlfriend without ever breaking up. He was in touch with his passionate nature and his needs on an intuitive level, but he could not verbally or honestly communicate this. Although he was his assisting his own personal survival, he was also burying his sense of self-worth.

Sometime in his childhood, he had most likely been "cut down" when he spoke the truth of his feelings. Now he was doing everything by evasion. He was evading the problem and just maneuvering its disappearance. If pushed, he would probably tell you that speaking up was too direct and could be "hurtful" to the other person, as well as shaming to him because he would have to explain his feelings. So, he took what seemed the easy way out, which was to just lose all of his belongings and financial security and no longer be the provider. He had to "lose" everything in order to walk away from a bad relationship.

My friend had managed to end the relationship, but his inability to truly "take the power," to speak up was still a very large part of his hidden feelings. This seemed to me a great dichotomy because when his band played, they performed on a stage in front of hundreds or thousands of people. There, *he* was the spokesperson for the band. To this grown man, speaking in front of these strangers was easy, while explaining his emotions to an intimate partner was absolutely frightening. He was somehow not allowed, not given permission to speak up for his own needs. And this frozen childhood restriction was still a part of his inner emotional make-up.

As you get in touch with your needs and wants, you can begin to "catch up" your early emotional self. With the help of your true inner passionate nature, you can avoid the predicament experienced by my musician friend.

DO YOU KNOW WHAT WORKS FOR YOU?

How do you deal with your problems? Do you believe that everything difficult or negative that happens comes from outside of you? If so, then you have no control over your life. However, if you understand that you are really the person in charge, then you can get in touch with the mechanisms you have created. When you change yourself, the problem can be released.

I once had a client who had married young, and when it did not work, he got divorced. He had no children and not many shared belongings, so the divorce itself was easy. But, the trauma of the divorce was not at all easy. My client sold everything he owned, packed up a small suitcase, left his job as a teacher and moved to another state about two thousand miles away. By moving, he had to give up his career because his teaching certificate was not recognized in the new state. Suddenly, he had no job, no new skills, few clothes and no belongings. He was like a ship set adrift in a vast uncharted ocean!

When he came to see me for counseling, he was without any purpose or goal and still reacting to the trauma of his divorce. Somehow, by divesting himself of all of his belongings, he felt that he had let go of his previous life. However, he had not created a new life for himself. He was out of touch with his passionate nature. When I asked what he wanted, he did not know. He knew only what *he did not want.*

We worked for a few months to get him in touch with what was really important and enjoyable. Once he had done this, he began to create a new life by picking and choosing what was enjoyable and had meaning. Now that he had replaced his emptiness with more fun, he could again have an identity and look forward to someday finding another true love.

When we experience a trauma, let go of old life patterns or significantly change our lives, we are forced to find new, meaningful goals. In finding the enjoyments that make life pleasurable, we discover our true selves and what we have come here to accomplish. Thus, to know yourself is to be able to please yourself, moving one step closer to your God Force nature. Relaxed and in touch with the universal level of your oneness, you can experience yourself in synch.

This is sort of like when you go to move your arm. You do not consciously think about moving your arm. You just tell it to move and it obeys your command. When you are in touch with your true passions, you begin to like yourself. You are comfortable in your own home because now you know what to expect. The added bonus is that once you really know *who* you are and what makes you tick, whatever you like, want and need automatically comes forward.

Animals have a knack of being in touch with their natural desires all of the time. Human beings are usually not so in tune and often create a barrier between their desires and actions. I call this the process of using the mind. Our minds are trained to tell us how to behave and what to do, which is a control mechanism that has been beneficial to civilization. But this also restricts us from getting in touch with and acting out our true passionate nature.

When lifting your foot to walk up the stairs, for example, you do not spend time understanding it with your mind. You just *will* your foot to lift. But often we are not so explicit with our needs and our inner passions. We discuss it with our mind and then deviate from what we really want. We squash our passions to fit into an image of what or how we *think* we should be. And so we create a separation between spirit and body, between our inner passions and our actions.

In short, we do what the animals do not do—act out of our mind. Then, we tell ourselves that we are special, a higher form of nature. Actually, we are merely creating ourselves to be instantaneously out of touch. The resulting division between feeling and action is the beginning of disease, that is, unhealthy, uncomfortable situations that become focused or stored in the body. This dichotomy of modern civilization has us working with no personal attachment to our jobs, relating without true connection to other people and functioning out of touch with our bodies. We are therefore in situations of stress that lead to apathy, boredom and dissatisfaction with life.

TAKING STOCK OF WHERE YOU STAND

If you believe or understand how you can create your own reality, then you will take the time to check-in with yourself and see what is happening. Checking-in with how you feel is learning to recognize whether or not you are in touch with your own passionate nature.

There are many ways to recognize when you are out of touch with your true nature. This is probably the case in the following scenarios:

1. If you lose your temper irrationally, a great deal of anger or unresolved emotion may be left over from a time when you did something you did not *really* want to do.

2. If you cry at the drop of a hat for no known reason or when someone says something nice to you, you may be craving love. If you cry when a person makes you feel wanted or needed or when someone gives you attention, perhaps you aren't giving yourself enough love. We all want to receive love, but until we give ourselves this love, we cannot follow our own passionate nature. Those "seeking" love on the outside are stuck in the approval phenomenon and often forsake what they feel for what another person wants.

3. If you let someone else always make your decisions for you, you are denying your passionate nature. Women often let their husbands make the decisions. You might agree with this idea, but also take time to consider important matters for yourself. Likewise, husbands often let their wives make all decisions about the household. Wherever you live, consider how things affect you and become some, if only a small, part of the decision-making process.

4. If you "down" yourself by not trusting in your own abilities to create the kind of life you want to have, then you are out of touch with your passionate nature. If you do not believe in yourself and lack self-esteem, then you are out of touch with your passionate nature.

5. If your fears are driving you, then you are not acting out of your passion. Controlled by fear, you are acting out of insecurity.

6. If you feel unhappy or unfulfilled, then you are definitely out of touch with your passionate nature on some level. The same goes for if you do not *like* your life as it is right now.

7. If you make everyone else feel good but you do not feel good, then you are out of touch with your feelings. If you are busy taking care of everyone else but not taking care of yourself, then you are definitely out of touch on some important level.

8. If nothing excites you, then you are not in touch with your passions. If you are bored, you're not living but simply existing. Life is more than just existing. Doing things that interest and fascinate you will create a *passion* to live!

9. If you feel that life has passed you by, you will need to remember your dreams.

10. If you are suicidal and want to just end things as they are, you are out of touch. This is also true if you are stuck and can see no way out of your problems. When in touch with your passion, however, you will always discover *some* way to overcome every predicament. Your passionate nature provides the creativity, desire and will power to *live* to your fullest potential.

11. If your sex life is nonexistent or you live mostly in fantasy, you are out of touch with your passionate nature.

12. If you repress your emotions 99 percent of the time and say there is no room for them, you are out of touch with your own intimate nature. This is also true if you are afraid *to feel*.

13. If you cannot make choices and do not know what you like, you are not in touch with your passionate nature. Get to know what food you like, your favorite music, most enjoyed sports, best way to enjoy a night on the town and what makes you feel good. You might not always have time to do everything, but you should know what makes you happy.

GETTING TO KNOW YOURSELF

It is very important to do the right thing for yourself. Most of us are trained by cultural rules and regulations to care for everyone around us instead. But caring properly for yourself means enjoying the "good life." When you do what really works for you, it makes you happy, healthy and well balanced. As a result, it is natural and easy also to take care of the people around you.

Often I ask clients what excites them. I ask about what they like to do or their favorite sport. You would be surprised at how many people don't know what they like to do when they are not working. Not knowing what food makes your taste buds feel quenched, not being in touch with what excites you, not being in touch with your feelings leads to boredom which soon results in apathy, depression and confusion. If you find yourself lacking focus and feeling, turn to Appendix A and follow the exercises for getting to know your true nature.

When not knowing what they want, many of my clients ask about what skills or good jobs they had in past lives. But past lives are just that—PAST. It is not your past but your present feelings that should determine what makes you feel connected with your life. Your life, right now, is for new challenges and for discovering your abilities in this new body. Part of your path is finding out what you came here to do, and to do it. Knowing yourself is the first part of the equation of nurturing the passion within.

Chapter 4
Identifying Your True Desires

Are you doing *everything but* what comes naturally? By doing what comes naturally, you will be in touch with your passionate soul. But most of us let parents, teachers, social concerns and other people come between who we are and what we do. This weakens our health, creativity and permission to accomplish our true goals in life. In this chapter, you will find suggested actions and practical examples to inspire a more natural you.

Who is making your decisions?

From reading people's auras, I have discovered that most people also have their mother, father, grandparents, teachers and even close friends within themselves. That is a pretty big crowd of "other people" in one's private universe. When it's time to make a decision, can you identify your true desires? Let me give an example of a man who had quite a time doing this:

A Japanese American client came to me wanting to change jobs. He wanted a regular job working for someone else, but his girlfriend was pushing for a high status job that would make a lot of money. His mother wanted him to get a job that represented security until retirement. And, his friends told him there were no jobs available in his field as a financial consultant. He used to have his own business, but his partner, who had supplied many of the clients, had left and so he was not doing well.

I looked at his energy and suggested he keep looking for the type of job he was trained for. But he insisted that despite his efforts, there were no such jobs available. He was adamant and resistant. So I suggested he consider what other skills he could use and then reassess himself. He did this and became an administrative manager, who by the way also prepared financial books for the company.

A year later, my client came back. Unhappy with his job, he was finally open to seeing why he was not getting what he really wanted in life. The new job had provided two significant situations in which he had "discovered" for himself what I had tried to explain. Finally, he began to understand why he had not followed his passion and had placed himself in an undesirable position.

First, he was being paid as a middle manager when in fact he was doing the financial books. That is, he was well qualified and could have been paid a much higher wage as a CPA or a bookkeeper. This meant that his boss was getting his financial advisor expertise for free. Second, he was working for a conservative, rather authoritarian American Japanese company without any vacation time. If he wanted a four-day vacation, he would have to quit, take his vacation and then apply to be rehired. What had seemed like security was instead a rigid, dead-end position.

My client asked himself *why* he had put himself into this situation? Through self-inquiry, he noticed that he was a people pleaser. To please his mother, he got a job that represented security, even though he did not really *like* the job. To please his girlfriend, he took a job that seemed to have status and a good steady wage. To please his friends, he agreed that there were no jobs available in his field. What he did not do, however, was please himself. Sometimes it is better to accept the challenge of struggling to get what you want rather than running to the next "easier" thing. If he had persevered in finding a position in his field, he would have had more security and a much higher wage, as well as the status he really deserved.

He later told me that there were indeed jobs for him. But he lacked self-esteem and certainty, which was why he had not continued to look. He also learned that his present boss represented his mother's authority. Because she had divorced when he was young and had single-handedly brought him up, she was a very strong authority symbol. So he had gone to work in a similar situation, where he would once again be told what to do. He had listened to everyone but himself. After observing his actions, however, he believed he could get the job he liked to do. He realized that he *had only to believe in himself and follow his true passion.*

My client had lived in Japan until he was six years old, at which time his mother divorced and moved to America. I clairvoyantly looked at his aura and saw an old program from when he was age five. It was a picture he had developed while at school. The energy message in this image told him always to be "one of the group," doing everything to be accepted. It also told him to please everyone so that he would be accepted. Now, here he was still acting like *the child* who wanted to be accepted. Children may be likeable and loveable, but they are powerless with adults. And so, in the business world, he had put himself in a position where he, being the child, was powerless.

Of course, this stored picture was simply energy that unconsciously affected him. Clairvoyants call this self-programming. He so strongly believed in pleasing that he did this with everyone. In social situations, he said what he felt would make people happy so that they would like him. There is nothing wrong with fitting in. Everyone wants to be loved and accepted by their peers and their family. But if you have programmed yourself to satisfy everyone *before* yourself, you will wake up one day and find yourself miserable. If you are last on the list to be satisfied, often you will *not* get satisfied at all!

The trick in life is to follow your passions while also pleasing everyone as best you can. However, following your true path should come first.

This is not selfishness, but simply basic survival. You need to make your own decisions. My client is now looking for a job that he likes to do and that has high status in his field, one in which he will make a good living, feel good about himself and be prosperous.

From watching my clients in action over the years, I now deeply believe that if you know what you want, you can indeed get it. The trick is in knowing what you *really* want. To help you with this, Appendix A includes many different exercises for finding the true you. If you follow your own true passion, as suggested in the following paragraphs, you will be doing the right thing.

HOLDING TO YOUR OWN PURPOSE

From the time we are very young, we must live up to the demands of other people. Living up to the demands of other people can be tedious and unrewarding. If you consistently give in to others' expectations, however, you may lose touch with your own true purpose.

I had a client in Tokyo whose father was a doctor. She had gone to medical school but was dissatisfied, so she switched to law studies instead. Her father was very upset by this choice because, historically, theirs was a family of doctors, not lawyers. He had reached the zenith of his career after having developed new procedures and techniques that he wanted her to carry on with. She listened patiently to her father and then came to see me for counseling.

My client was young, but she knew instinctively that she would not enjoy the field of medicine. If she continued as a doctor, she would be doing this only to please her father and her relatives. Traditionally, she felt that she should comply, but internally she knew that being a doctor was not her true soul nature.

As a counselor, I cannot make decisions for people. I can only point them in their own direction. So I asked what she really wanted to do, deep within herself. She answered that she wanted to be a lawyer. This was a difficult decision because it seemed to go against all of her traditional standards. I suggested that if she decided not to be a doctor, she could apologize to her father for not being what he wanted. She could tell him that perhaps her future children (his grandchildren) would continue his work, but it was not within her to do this.

You are given a special path in life, which you must strive to find. If you go off of your path to fulfill another person's dream, you create karma both for yourself and with everyone around you. Although it can be difficult, it is important to follow the dictates of your own soul pattern, even when this goes against your current tradition. The nature of your soul supersedes the dictates of tradition because it is your highest essence. Try to live up to your highest potential spiritually while you are here in this body. Acting out of your true passionate soul nature is the highest level of development to which you can aspire.

MAINTAINING YOUR ENERGETIC SPACE

Finding your true passion is not just finding what makes you feel in touch with yourself. It is also a process of tuning out everyone else's ideas. Clairvoyants call this "owning your space." This means owning your own private universe, which is your aura, the electromagnetic energy surrounding your body like a giant, ethereal multicolored egg. Even though you may not see your energy self, it protects you and also holds the information of who you are and what you do. In other words, it is your instant book of life. To a clairvoyant, it can clearly and instantaneously reveal your inner nature and how you express your personality.

When someone steps too close or a stranger touches you, it may feel like an invasion of your space. The immediate personal space surrounding you is your sphere of influence, your comfort zone. People can invade this physically, as they often do on a crowded train or bus even when it is not done purposefully. People can also invade your space emotionally, mentally or energetically. When friends give you their emotional problems to solve, they invade your space. When parents, relatives or teachers leave you with thoughts that tell you what to do, they are invading your space. And when a spiritual cult or group tries to plan your life, they are invading your space. It is important to recognize your own space and always have a comfort zone on physical, emotional, mental and spiritual levels.

Do you realize that your universe is your private creative space? As captain of your ship and master of your universe, you need to make critical decisions based on what *you* need. We may all be very similar or have similar goals and desires, but we are also very different. Because everyone is unique, we all have slightly different needs. The quality of your life is related to your ability to act out of the true feelings of your private universe.

Let's do a little exercise. Sit down and close your eyes and create an image of your own private universe. Who is there? Where are you, and what are you doing? Is anyone in there with you? Whatever is in your private universe energetically is also being created in the outer "real" world. See what you have created. If you find other people, rules and regulations or things not of your making, take them out. Whenever things do not work for you, sit down and close your eyes. Create your life the way you want it to be. The "real" external world will mirror what you create in your private universe.

DESERVING A BETTER LIFE

I believe that if you are on your true path, you will always be in touch enough to do the right thing. However, many people have a lot of confusion about how to be true to themselves and also be there for family and friends, work and religious duties. Being true to yourself is living up to your highest potential as a member of the human race. It is not about being selfish or self-centered. We do not always put ourselves first, nor last either, but we do what is best for *all* involved in every situation.

Often we shortchange ourselves by having low self-esteem. If you believe you don't "deserve" something, then you act accordingly. Sometimes when you feel undeserving, your body language tells people not to offer you something. For example, I had a client who married a young man who did not believe he was capable at his job. He and my client had a child and their expenses increased. She needed her husband to make more money, but he was continually passed over for promotions. Finally, my client looked at her husband as if he were a stranger while she tried to assess him. She saw that he held his body stiffly and kept it too much to himself. He seemed to shrink when speaking and to move away from the person to whom he was speaking. This made others uncomfortable. It also created a situation in which they did not naturally trust him. In business, this made him seem weak or removed.

"What should I do," she asked? The two of us brainstormed about what would change her husband in the fastest manner. The next week, she took him to a high quality tailor, who prepared some fine, expensive suits. She taught him to stand straight and showed him how to breathe and relax when meeting new people. She introduced him to exercises that pulled his shoulders back and told him to repeat certain jokes in his head whenever he wanted to disappear or get away from people.

When you feel like leaving a situation but cannot, your body language will often show it. You can circumvent this lack of self-esteem by repeating in your mind certain affirmations. My client's preparation soon paid off and her husband got a raise, made more friends at the office and improved their marital relationship as well. I am sure you know the saying, "Clothes make the man." Nevertheless, this was not the whole story. Many things were combined to deliver a better image and a finer life. Her husband wanted to be successful but "feared" he did not deserve it. She showed him how to circumvent his fear and to act from his powerful inner self.

You might want to take the time to reassess yourself. If you cannot be neutral about yourself, write down a few key questions and have your friends, relatives, coworkers and associates give you feedback. It is not that difficult to make simple, yet striking, changes that can express your true inner soul to the world. Learning to believe in yourself is learning to act from inner feelings. It is learning to empower yourself to deserve the best of life.

UNDERSTANDING YOUR MORAL PROGRAMMING

Every culture has its share of moral programming, and every generation within a culture has its own version of how to carry out that morality. As a clairvoyant, I believe that moral programming is set by humanity, not by God. If you are in touch with your inherent God-like nature, you will always do the right thing in a situation. If you have to live by rules and regulations, it is because you do not believe in your inherent goodness.

Rules are guidelines that teach compassion to the children and give a basic idea of how to behave in the community. As adults evolve spiritually, they become naturally responsible within themselves. Of course, we have laws for people who are "not in touch" and might cause harm to others. Many people, though, create an extra moral system to legislate their moral values to themselves. Instead of naturally facing a decision, they devise their own set of regulations. Often these inner rules are so overbearing that they restrict normal movement within one's life.

Take the time to find out about any moral programs within yourself. Are they truly yours, or do they belong to your parents or relatives? If they are yours, do you feel they are necessary? If they are someone else's, do they really represent you or have you merely inherited them? If you are not happy with your moral program or do not need it, you might consider getting rid of it. The exercises in Appendix A demonstrate how to release unnecessary moral programs.

RELEASING NEGATIVE SELF-PROGRAMMING

Do you do things just because you feel that you "should"? When you act simply because you feel it is the proper thing to do, a part inside of you is not in agreement with your actions. If you do this type of thing often, a whole part of you becomes estranged or separate from your conscious self. You become out of touch with your inner feelings and may wake up one day unhappy or totally bored with everything in life. You can release all "shoulds" and begin doing things because you really want to. This makes you feel good and feeds your passionate soul.

Take a moment to look at your own self-programming. Do you find yourself saying any of the phrases listed here? Do you bend your actions to fit into everyone else's life? Do you restrict yourself to just being there for everyone else? The following are examples of self-programming that can defeat you:

If I do this, even though I do not enjoy it, I will look good and have status.

If I do this, even though I do not enjoy it, I will fit in.

If I do this, even though I do not enjoy it, I will make more money.

If I do this job, I will please people (parents, friends, etc.).

This is the most responsible thing to do.

Doing this job makes me a good person.

Going to the movie my friend wants to see makes me a good friend.

This is the way everyone else does it. I am supposed to do it this way.

If you say these inner commands to yourself and follow them, you will want to answer the following questions:

What do I *feel* when I do this?

Does this make me feel satisfied and responsible?

Does doing this make me feel good?

Do I still feel conflict within myself?

When you do something that is not your inner passionate nature, it creates a personal conflict that does not go away. Over time, this can create an imbalance so that you are not happy or at peace. Suddenly, you are acting out of everyone else's needs and not listening to your own. You become a soul lost to yourself. If this is the case, you will want to read the next chapter to understand how to possess your own passionate soul.

MAKING YOUR DECISIONS WITH AWARENESS

Who *really* makes your life decisions? You might be essentially one person, but there are many aspects or different types of behavior within yourself. Psychologists often categorize people's aspects into three categories: child, adult and parent. As a child, you are open to everything, naive and loving but powerless to make decisions unless you have the experience and help of an adult. As an adult, you are the breadwinner (the worker), serious, responsible and in charge. As a parent, you are caring and always responsible for taking care of everyone.

When you make a decision, do you hear your mother's or father's voice inside your head telling you what is best? Do you hear your friends telling you what works for them? Is your teacher's information more important than your own? Who is really making your decisions? Are they based on your inner passion?

Take a moment to look at when you are the child, the adult or the parent. If you are the child at work or in a relationship, then you have no personal power in that situation. If you are always the adult, then you have no permission to play as the child does. If you are the parent in every situation (at work, at home, in your primary relationship, with friends), then you are always taking care of everyone.

See if you are balanced or if you spend more time being just one of these categories. There is always time to be the child and play, to be the adult and work and to be the parent and care. If you are balanced, you can be all three. However, we are usually one of these more often than the other two. Take a few moments to understand yourself and which aspect of you is uppermost in important situations. Appendix B has exercises for discovering whether you are the child, adult or parent. It also has quick methods for recognizing who is really making your decisions.

CREATING THE WIN-WIN SITUATION

To have your true passion in life, you do not have to give up something. Sometimes you just have to figure out how to put all your desires together in one package. I call this the win-win situation.

I had a client in America who had a great dichotomy in life. He sold real estate, which he really enjoyed. But one day, he discovered the game of golf. He was so enamored with this game that he began to practice all the time, and after a while he soon found himself neglecting his real estate business.

My client asked if there was some way he could find a job that would include golf. He did not have enough funding to purchase a golf course. Of course, he was not accomplished enough to be a golf instructor, and most of the other related jobs were not lucrative enough to support him and his family. Further, he was not interested in being the turf keeper or a golf caddy. He just had this great desire to be on the golf course most of the time.

I simply suggested the most logical path to him. He could do his real estate deals mostly on the golf course. Meanwhile, an assistant could do more of the office work and paper details. I suggested that he could show a property and then discuss the sale while playing golf. He followed my suggestion and today he is happy in his thriving real estate business, and his golf game is much better. This man found creative ways to enjoy his true passion.

Finally, to create the best outcome, it is important to set realistic goals. If you do not live up to your own expectations and "disappoint" yourself, you can soon lose faith in yourself. You also lose self-esteem when you reject your own abilities.

When you see a challenge that is a little difficult but that you want to accomplish, does your inner voice say, "You can do this"? If you are always thinking, "No way can I do this," then you have expectations of yourself that are too high. To succeed, change your expectations to something you believe is realistic, and you will find that you like yourself more. It is good to create a number of positive affirmations you can say in the face of challenges or difficult situations. To make life work well, be your own cheerleader.

Chapter 5
The Energy Anatomy of Freedom

Your individuality, the essence of your true soul nature, is a gift. This divine essence is the true cosmic nature of your soul reflecting your ability to learn lessons in life. Each person's unique difference produces the creative geniuses that change our world. However, most early childhood training teaches us to conform, to be the same as everyone else and not to rock the boat. Unfortunately, this repetitive type of "memorize and regurgitate" learning that typically comprises the school system does not give us permission to learn and grow. We begin to repeat only what we are taught, forgetting to think and act creatively. Thus, generations of students are bored with themselves, thinking they have to accept a lower version of their life dream. To have a strong society and equally strong country, we need to give ourselves permission to shift into a new mode of behavior, the behavior of freedom.

Just what is freedom? From a clairvoyant view, freedom is not being controlled by another person's energy, programs or morality, but acting out of one's innate emotional, moral and energetic nature. Why and how do we lose our freedom in the first place? First we get out of touch with ourselves by following everyone else's programs. Second, we lose touch with what we are all about by not understanding our own energy system.

POSSESSING YOUR OWN SOUL

My friend had a good job as a public relations supervisor in a medium-size company. He was a happy person who enjoyed life, but everyone remarked that he had much more capability and pizzazz than he was using in his job. They saw him as an underachiever, overqualified for a job where no one expected much at all. His boss asked only that he satisfy customers and make them feel good. My friend, however, was a very smart man who had studied both medicine and psychology. He was not a doctor or a psychologist, but an astute businessman well versed in human nature. Moreover, he was not knowledgeable about himself. It was true that his job was too easy. He was bored and didn't know it. But everyone else did!

Finally, a client from a large corporation came by asking for a person in management and wondered whether my friend would be interested. When he checked in with himself and his feelings, he discovered that he was feeling unwanted, unneeded, unappreciated and generally not comfortable at work. So, he quit and joined the larger corporation. From day one, he was given work that was a constant challenge and was praised when he did well. He thrived at his new job.

A few months later, I asked why he had worked for four years at a job that was not a challenge. He said, "Well, I knew that I was overqualified, but it was really *easy*. Everyone kept telling me how lucky I was that I had a job with absolutely no pressure to perform! My father had always been stressed out at work by trying to do well, so he thought this was wonderful for me. But, I'm not like my father at all. I discovered that I like a little stress. I thought my father knew best, but I am really different."

My friend had lost touch with his own passionate self and what made him excited. He had listened to everyone else when he should have listened only to his inner self. Once he turned himself around and possessed his own soul, his life took off. He became excited and everything fell into place.

Not everyone has the luck to realize, soon enough, that they are in the wrong job, or the wrong apartment or the wrong relationship. Sometimes a person has to work to get in touch with true inner needs. If you are questioning your choices, try looking at some of the exercises in Appendix A to get in touch with what you really feel. By doing this you can make an informed decision about creating the quality of life you want to have.

ACTING FROM YOUR OWN DESIRES

It is easy to look at historical events, such as World War II, and see how an entire population in one country was mesmerized or controlled by an individual or a common belief system. Of course, hindsight makes it obvious that either the financial times or the social system was at work. For example, because every person was under the shadow of one dynamic individual who could react to the agonies of the time, this man was able to influence a mass action that led to personal and political disaster for many.

Most people, however, do not look at the manner in which we are constantly bombarded and influenced on a personal level by other people's energy or belief systems. Have you ever asked yourself why you do something that you obviously do not want to do? When does this occur? Do you act out of guilt, responsibility, a need to please? Or, do you just feel someone else's desires influencing you more strongly than your own?

I believe that, on some level, we are completely aware when doing something contrary to our own desires. We feel it when we ignore our true passion, but many people have an overriding program that does not pay attention to their own needs. Take a moment to look at a time when you acted out of someone else's desires instead of your own. What did you feel when you carried out someone else's needs? Why did you ignore your own true feelings? Do you still do this with the same person?

Some years ago, I had a friend named Jasmine, who had an office job. It was an okay job, but it did nothing special for her life other than to pay the rent and put food on her table. One day while chatting with her, she confided, "My mother has always wanted me to have a steady, reliable income until I marry. Her dream for me is to work in an office, but that really bores me. I do not want to disappoint my mother, but I need to do my own thing, too."

Jasmine was young, single and adventurous. In her spare time, she collected stories written by women for women. One day as I sat in her kitchen drinking tea, she told me about how, with a very small amount of money, she had created a small journal of women's erotic fiction. This excited her. Her eyes almost glowed, her skin blushed with health and she looked happy. Reading erotic stories is not really my cup of tea, but I did my best to support Jasmine in what enchanted her. This obviously was her true passion.

When I saw Jasmine at a party about a year later, she looked happier than ever before. "How is it going?" I asked.

"I've quit my job," she beamed. "My magazine has a large subscription now. It supports me and I really like doing it all day. It's lots of fun. Doing my erotic journal might be a little risky, but it makes every day exciting."

As I walked around the party speaking to people, I began to realize that Jasmine had become a homegrown celebrity. She was the first woman to do this type of magazine, and many other women found it interesting and titillating. Jasmine had obviously found her niche. She had created a career by following her passion. I am sure that even though her mother was "afraid" for Jasmine's financial independence, she was also proud of Jasmine's success. Jasmine had stopped behaving like her mother and started following her own dream.

If you start to understand why you carry out another person's wishes above your own, you will understand your true motivation. You will understand how to recognize what you want and steer yourself toward your true goal instead.

KNOWING THE NATURE OF YOUR OWN ENERGY

You are endowed with a certain amount of energy, which gives you a lift in the morning and sustains you throughout the day. It is essentially your life force, which is imprinted with your personal patterns and programs. When other people attempt to control you or enforce their reality upon you, they often move their personal energy into your space.

Your comfort zone, the area close to you that is your own environment, is your personal universe. When others step into that area, they are being either intimate or invasive. If someone should hug or kiss you, he is being intimate. If you like this and enjoy the hug or kiss, you will enjoy the closeness and feel comfortable. If you are on a train at rush hour and have to stand so close to people that they are directly in touch with your body, you will usually be uncomfortable. When strangers stand too close, they are in your comfort zone. When people threaten you or challenge you to a fight, they often invade your comfort zone. Environmentally, your apartment is your comfort zone. At work, your office or desk area is your comfort zone. On a bus, your seat is your comfort zone. On a personal level, your comfort zone is usually the area that surrounds your body two feet in every direction.

Your energy contains your own personal programs. If another person enters your space and leaves her energy, then essentially she is dumping her programs into your computer. These programs, however, do not work well in your computer. Another person's programs are mostly alien to you and eventually produce confusion as you move to avoid them. Or, you may freeze up while making decisions because another's programs give you information contradictory to your wants and needs.

Your energy is created for you. It alone holds the essential blueprint for you in this life. Someone else's energy can disrupt your flow of information by feeding you an alien program. Accepting another person's moral or conceptual identity leads either to a loss of energy or an actual possession of your identity and functions.

Most people can notice when they are being invaded by another person's energy. Suddenly, they act out of character and feel emotions they know are not theirs. Often they feel sick or confused or find themselves acting out another's addictive behavior. If you take some time to be in touch with yourself, through meditation or simply getting to know yourself and your actions, you will be able to recognize when a foreign energy is driving you.

Sometimes, however, it takes some help to realize what a strong influence another person's energy can be. For example, once I had a client who had been in a relationship with one man for about eight years. She and he were definitely a couple. They were always together and seemed to get along very well. Their parents on both sides expected them to marry soon. One day, my client told me that although she loved her boyfriend, she had come to the conclusion that she was not IN love. She enjoyed being with him, but did not feel any passion for him as a man.

"How long have you felt this way?" I asked.

"For about seven and a half years," she confessed.

This was almost as long as the relationship had existed. I wondered why she continued to go out with this man if she was not really in love. At first she did not answer and got very quiet, almost withdrawing into herself. Then she started speaking quickly, as if all of her feelings and thoughts had to come out and be released all at once.

She said, "My parents really like him. He is kind and good company. All of my friends think we make a great couple. Everyone says we were made for one another!"

"But what do you feel?" I quizzed.

"I feel that I like him. I guess I am confused. I feel we *should* be good together."

"Are you good together?"

She looked sad and I could see tears forming in her eyes. "We have fun, and for me we are like good friends. But Jimmy, he really loves me, and I just have never felt the same way back."

"Does he know this?"

"I think that he does on some level. But he does not want to face it. I have made my decision. I want to leave him. It just is not right!"

"Do you have a problem leaving?" I asked.

"Every time I want to leave, I keep hearing voices in my head. I hear my mother telling me what a perfect husband he will be—he went to the right school, has a good job, is a responsible man. I hear my friends saying how wonderful we are as a couple, how good we look together. I hear my father telling me that I will have good healthy children with him. I know we should break up, but I'm afraid! Everyone else thinks it is so right."

For five sessions, we discussed her true feelings about Jimmy. I showed her some energy skills for moving out the "voices" of her mother, her father and her friends. I explained how we often let loved ones *program* us to do what they feel is right. That is, when people emotionally possess you, you may be acting out of *their* feelings instead of your own. I also taught her skills for releasing emotional possession and guilt so she could act on her own feelings. Two months after our last session, she and Jimmy parted as a couple. Soon after, she met a young man that she was very attracted to. They eventually married and are still happily married today.

AVOIDING THE "GIVER" TRAP

Pleasing people is one way to take on another's personal view of the world. To be accepted or loved, or just to fit in, you may become a "giver." The giver is always doing something for someone else. He or she "gives" so that others will eventually give back. Unfortunately, this does not always happen. Often, people who are "given to" just accept what is given and do not see a need to return the favor. On a material level, when someone gives a gift, we usually feel obliged to give something in return. But energetically, with emotions in tow, we may not see a need to please the person who has helped us.

Notice whether you are pleasing someone just because you want to be loved or accepted. Many times, people will change their entire dress and behavior to make someone else happy. I have seen a client change her hairstyle to suit a new man friend. Then she goes on to dress according to his taste, eat food that he likes and even remove from her diet anything he dislikes. Although women seem to overplease in response to lifestyle influences, men often do this type of pleasing toward a boss or male authority figure. And, I have witnessed both sexes appear shell shocked upon getting a divorce and discovering they have spent an entire marriage being who they are not.

Do you say or do things that do not come from your own inner soul? It is common in business not to rock the boat. So when a client says he just loves this music or that food, often everyone else will agree. In this situation, you know that you are agreeing just temporarily. But if you continually adjust your tastes and behavior to fit your mate, to make him or her more comfortable, you may be losing your true soul connection. Once you are untrue to yourself, you develop a conflict that creates poor self-esteem within your own system. You can live with a mate, please that person and share enjoyed moments without shifting your entire soul nature to be someone else's vision of perfection. You do not have to give up your entire self to please people, and if you do this you should check out why you do it.

CREATING NEW TRADITIONS THAT WORK

One of my clients was torn between love and respect for her father, who wanted her to work in the family business, and her own inner need to excel as an artist. All of her father's children worked in the company. Matter of fact, all of her extended relatives worked there. From the time she was a child, however, she had felt a need to draw, paint and design. To be a "good" daughter, however, she wanted to follow her father's wishes. But to be a well-balanced person, follow her passionate soul and fulfill her karmic path, she had to act out of her true nature and be an artist.

If this young woman tried to "do the right thing" according to her relatives, she would probably be miserable for the rest of her work life. So, we have to ask ourselves why tradition is often not in alignment with our true nature. Perhaps the way we are in touch with our traditions is changing in this modern age. We may need to change our idea that tradition is a primary point from which to make major life decisions.

Sets of rules and beliefs protect family and societal values. Slowly, but surely, the values of older cultures are changing, however. Although being the same and fitting in worked before World War II, we are shifting or rewriting our values in the new millennium. The ability to use individual creativity, to change and improve systems around us, to create scientific inventions and methodologies, innovative businesses and new ways of doing things is more in tune with the current technological milieu of this century.

You will, therefore, have to "search your soul" when you need to make a decision that pits you between tradition and doing what really works for you. Try to remember that tradition exists to make you and your society strong. If instead you are following a role by rote, thus making yourself weak, perhaps traditional ways are not correct or workable in your situation.

Preserving your energetic freedom

In truth, you and you alone are responsible for your actions. When you accept someone else's authority over your own, you could be allowing that person to make decisions for you. But, you are still responsible for your own life. So, it is always wise to listen to another's advice, but in the end, make your own decisions.

I have noticed something over the years. When people study with a teacher, they often seem to think that a teacher expert in one thing is an expert in everything. But, a person who cooks well cannot always be the person who can handle your financial affairs. Likewise, a teacher who plays the piano or loves tennis is not always the best relationship counselor. To believe that an expert in one department is an expert in all things does not work. In fact, it can lead to cult behavior.

When we accept someone else's authority in making decisions for us, it is usually because we are still looking for approval from mother or father. This dependency on substitute parental authority figures can happen at work, in a spiritual organization and with a parent-like neighbor, friend or teacher. Part of "growing up" is stepping away from parents and becoming the parent or adult in our own right, that is, by taking enough responsibility to be our own authority. Some people are "grown up" at age seventeen and others have not yet accomplished this at seventy. However, becoming an adult is not so much a matter of age as a choice to accept ownership.

When your passionate soul tries to live someone else's dream, you are in danger of stepping off your true path. Losing your passionate soul is much more serious than becoming bored, deadened or out of touch with life. It can actually be losing the precious connection with your soul essence, the part that aligns you with universal life force. Therefore, losing touch with your passionate soul can lead to sickness, disease, an unconscious absence of the will to live and an inability to communicate well with other people. The absence of this very germ of life, the built-in incentive that Mother Nature gives you as the will to live fully, can block the joy of truly doing what you came here to do!

To prevent the loss of your energetic freedom, you simply need to do three things:

1. Get to know yourself. Experience what you really feel on a passionate soul level and what you really want and need in life.

2. Discover and acknowledge when and how you give away your right to make your own decisions. Then you will be able to recognize and prevent being incorrectly influenced when it happens.

3. Give permission to love yourself enough to always do "the right thing" for yourself. In other words, you have to come to terms with righteous selfishness, which is enacting the karmic lesson you came here to accomplish—even if it is not respected, loved, acknowledged, liked or approved of by your friends and family.

When you freely act out the passionate nature of your soul, you truly have the most to give. As you are more in touch with your true nature, others receive permission from your drive and charisma to follow their true nature as well. It is as if the shining light of your inner fire sparks everyone else.

Chapter 6
Overcoming Insecurities

We are all insecure some of the time. This is why we have rules and regulations, traditions and belief systems, morality issues and commitments to institutions. When we are insecure, our fears rule us. If you learn to face your fears and thus remove the reason for insecurity, you can live your life in freedom. You will avoid being a slave to everyone else's ideas of what is right and wrong.

Insecurity leads to overcontrol

What are our insecurities and how do they manifest? My husband was an excellent cleaner at home. He could wash a kitchen counter so it was immaculate or wash a bunch of glasses so they would sparkle. But he would wash the kitchen counter or the glasses *only* when he was upset. For example, if something went wrong at work or if he had an argument with his brother, he would use his energy washing or cleaning to "control" his environment.

When you feel a loss of control, you may try to overcontrol your immediate environment. Executives do the same thing in their offices. When something is not going right, they will start to organize their desk. Suddenly, every stack of paper is even and every pencil and pen is in its proper place. Insecurity causes us to fear change, and so we try to regulate the present as much as possible.

Many of my business clients are insecure at work and tend to overcontrol other workers. These clients are usually managers or CEOs, who know their job from top to bottom but do not trust this job to others. They resist delegating power and try to do everything alone. Obviously, this doesn't pay because it takes teamwork to make a company run smoothly. I usually point out their insecurities and remind them to allow their workers to do what they were hired to do. These managers need to move beyond their insecurities and learn to let go.

SAYING WHAT YOU FEEL

Insecurities can crop up all over the place in your life. For example, are you unsure to the point of squelching your passion? Are you able to verbalize your true feelings? I have a friend who just got divorced and is dating new men. When she meets someone she likes, she wonders how much to say to him. She calls and wonders if she should tell him that she likes him. Then, she might ask, "Should I suggest that he take me to a concert of the kind of music we both like?" before countering, "Or, should I wait for him to suggest it?"

I once had a friend who fell deeply in love with a man she had dated for five months. She called me every night for weeks asking similar yet even more pointed questions. "Should I tell him that I love him?" she would fret over the phone at midnight after getting back from her date. "Or should I wait until he tells me first?"

Beginning love relationships really bring out the quakes in people. My friend's scenario would run like this: "If I tell him I love him and he does not fell the same, I will feel lost and rejected and hurt and embarrassed. If I do not tell him I love him, maybe he'll find some other lady who will tell him and he'll go off with her. But if he loves me, why doesn't he tell me?"

One day her boyfriend said something that suggested he loved her. Before he could say another word, she broke down and blurted out that she loved him, and then he finally said the same thing. A few months later they were married. I often speculate what would have happened if each had held out, never saying the *love* word. Would they have stayed together, innately recognizing their love? Or, would they have eventually gone off with other people who were more direct?

When you verbalize your passion, it gives a special power of owning your feelings. Being outspoken frees you from hiding from the other person and allows you to express yourself. This is most often releasing and liberating. Even if the other person does not reply in agreement, you no longer carry the burden of pent up feelings.

DEVELOPING YOUR TRUE ABILITIES

Sometimes insecurities keep us afraid to develop our own abilities. But, how do we get free? One of my clients has a childhood friend she had not seen in a while. "We got together and exchanged all the things that had happened during the years we were apart," she told me. "My friend is married now, but she doesn't look so happy."

"Why not?" I asked.

"Her husband is very conservative and doesn't want her to work. They have no children, so she stays at home all day."

I was curious. "What does she do at home?"

"She cleans. She cleans the house and then recleans it because she has nothing else to do."

"It must be a very clean house," I said diplomatically. My client frowned, so I inquired, "Can't she join a charity and do some community work?"

"Oh, traditional men don't want their women doing anything. Their wives are to be waiting there to take care of them."

"But he's not at home until quite late!" I exclaimed, not hiding my own perspective.

"I know," she answered. "But it makes some men very insecure if their wife gets involved in something that could take attention away from them."

This husband has prevented his wife from exploring her own passionate soul by insisting she serve his needs and insecurities. She, of course, has allowed him to restrain her from developing her own abilities. Even if she were to have children and would stay home caring for them, her inner passion would likely be muted because of his previous restraint. Deep inside, she might have some resentment toward him. Later in their relationship, this could come out in a destructive, unconscious manner. Further, by ignoring his wife's potential and blocking her natural passion, this man has created a situation that might someday come back to plague him. If his wife cannot verbalize her displeasure, then the communication between them is bound to be shallow or less honest.

Nevertheless, we cannot lay blame upon one person in such relationships because "It takes two to tango." Even though a husband requests that his wife stay home, in most cases she can initiate taking more responsibility, discuss her feelings with him and come to some agreement that is more freeing for her.

DOING WHAT YOU WANT TO DO

When a man acts out of his insecurities and tries to control his wife or home, he is acting out of fear. When a woman stays at home, even though she really doesn't want to, she is acting out of guilt, morality and responsibility. She is doing what her husband wants, what her parents think is "proper" and what she believes is her responsibility. Now, many times you have to, and *want to*, do the "proper" thing, the "responsible" thing, by acting with the correct moral behavior. But many times it is totally self-defeating to do something just because you feel guilty.

Clairvoyants have a saying that "Guilt is like a rocking chair. It moves a lot but goes nowhere." When you feel guilty, you are not acting out of love or according to your true inner feelings. When you are acting from this useless emotion, you cannot really help someone. You may be trying to make up for something you did in the past or wanting "to make it right," but inevitably you are not acting because you feel good about doing it. In short, feeling bad is not the right reason for doing it at all.

Guilt is an emotion that is not in harmony with your soul. If you doubt this, then try to remember when someone did something for you out of guilt. You will notice how poorly it makes you feel even though the person was doing something for you. When you get in touch with your inner passionate nature, you will always act out of love.

What does it mean to be moral? Moral codes are set up by someone— whether a person, institution, nation or culture. These are values-based guidelines created to control people who we believe would otherwise do bad or terrible things. There is something very sad about having to "set up" a moral code for someone to live by. This means that we think some folks have to be told what is right. If you are true to your soul and follow your true passionate nature, however, you should always do the right thing. When you doubt this truth, you end up following someone else's elaborate and sometimes rigid rules or traditions.

Your morality needs to be the expression of your soul, which comes from within and is expressed in love. If you act just to please others, you are not really in touch with your own feelings. This means you are not fully alive. You could devise your own inner moral code, but this may become such a mental point of perfection that you could get stuck. So, all in all, it is best to leave morality to your Higher Self, your true soul nature.

Responsibility includes the act of taking care of others. When we get out of touch with ourselves, being responsible feels like something we *have* to do. But true responsibility is done because you really *want* to.

Next time you feel you have to do something out of responsibility, find the part of you that *really* wants to "respond." Then you will be in touch with your inner passionate nature. And yes, especially when there are family responsibilities, usually some part of you *really* does want to do this.

REDUCING FEAR AND THE "I AM" STATE OF BEING

When people lose control and feel insecure, they are acting out of fear. Women who are fearful usually retreat within themselves. That is, we can be overemotional and dysfunctional. In contrast, men who are not in control often experience anger. This is common among men who have retired, for instance. They may sit at home feeling useless and try to find meaning in life. They look for something important to do or inwardly criticize themselves for everything through the years that they think didn't go well.

Babies are unable to care for themselves and must depend on others. Likewise, our elders need help for simple everyday survival at the end of the life spectrum. However, we do not like to admit that in between babyhood and old age, we are still not in control. Truly, we are never in total control. Even as adults, we need to go with the flow, to find our true power.

Thus, always needing to be in control can destroy your health and self-esteem, creating fear and stress. When we learn to go with the flow, we are able to give and receive love easily because we operate from our true essence. Life can be likened to riding the trains. You can be smart and aware enough to find the schedule and to know which train to ride, but you are never in control of what happens to the train or exactly where you will stand or sit or what type of ride you will have.

Are you always trying to be in control? Do you insist that areas of your home stay exactly the way you left them? Do you clean compulsively? Are you a neat freak? Do you get upset when people do not do what you think is right or correct? Are you a perfectionist? Do you plan everything? If you do any of these things, you are likely trying to control your world from the mindset of insecurity. To end the fear syndrome, accept everything just the way it is. Of course, you can create order and have a clean house. But enjoy life and enjoy being just the way you are, right now in the present moment.

Spiritually, this concept is known as the "I Am" state of being. You are always moving and changing, trying to improve yourself and your life, but right now you can also be in the moment. You are the best of who you are right now. "I Am" suggests that you love yourself just the way you are. Without thoughts, bask in the inner space of allowing yourself to be. You are acting out your life purpose without trying to understand or control it. And when you do this, there is no fear. If you want to access the "I Am" experience, check out the exercises in Appendix A.

HELPING THE BODY FEEL LOVED AND SUPPORTED

I have a friend who is a "touchy feely" person. He visited my home a few weeks ago because we were doing some business together. Ralph is a grandfather who also owns a busy medium-size design business, where he manages a lot of employees. What is interesting about Ralph is that he used to be a fireman and an emergency medical person (one of those people who rides with ambulances). We have had many long telephone discussions about his experience in the field. Ralph tells me stories about people who have died in his arms. He has had incredible visions that have come true about the people he has cared for at various accident sites. Ralph is what clairvoyants call "an old soul." He intuitively understands how to calm people, how to reach their inner nature and how to bring them immediately into a sense of balance.

As we walked in my garden, I suddenly realized what was different about communicating with Ralph. First, let me explain that I spend at least twelve days of every month in Japan. While I am there, I am comfortable and at home, as if it were my own culture. It is not my culture, but I enjoy Japanese music and the Japanese way of doing things. I instinctively have no problems with the typical Japanese manner of greeting, which is bowing.

Moreover, I am comfortable with the fact that Japanese people do not touch. In the States, we are a hodgepodge of people from all different cultures. Here, we have the tradition of shaking hands as a common greeting, to which we all behave differently depending on our cultural upbringing and the occasion. In business the world over, most people do not "touch" one another physically, even though on a personal level there are many ways of touching or not touching. For example, Ralph was brought up to touch people.

As I spoke to Ralph, I noticed that he touched me all of the time. He touched my arm, my elbow and my shoulder. Now, I was brought up with a traditional, European way of relating, and our family members never touched one another. I remember the first time I became aware of my parents actually hugging me. That was the day they took me to my college dorm and were saying goodbye. They were releasing me to go on as a college student, to grow up and make my dreams in life.

I remember how powerfully emotional I felt inside. I wondered why they had never hugged me before or told me so strongly that they loved me. Why had they waited until I was leaving to tell me they really cared? Once in college, I discovered that many of my dorm mates had been "hugged and loved" continuously throughout childhood. They seemed more comfortable with their bodies and their emotions. And so, for the first two years of college, I worked to allow myself to feel comfortable with "touchy feely huggy" people as well as with people who never touched. I really worked to let go of the fear I had around my body. I tried to release the insecurity that had developed from never being told I was loved. I intentionally took on a feeling that love surrounded both my body and me and that everything I did or said would come from a loving, supportive place.

Touching, whether physical or emotional, is a very private act. As a woman, I have always been sensitive about who stands close to or who touches me, especially when it comes to men. If a man touches me while doing business or having a personal conversation and there is the slightest sexual overtone (and if I am NOT interested in that), I will quickly and permanently be sure to place space between my body and his. Therefore, I found myself having an unusual experience in the garden with Ralph. He must have touched me at least twenty times. And yes, I started to count because suddenly I began having a reaction to his touch. Just back from Japan a few days before, I was used to speaking with people on a warm, heart level (many Japanese are marvelously open, heartfelt people) without ever physically touching or being touched. And here was this man touching me at every moment.

But Ralph's touches were not sexual in any way. He was being intimate, but not intimate as a man to a woman. He was being intimate as one soul speaking to another soul. Each time he touched me, he was reminding me that I was a special being in a body and that my body was precious and alive. He was reminding me that I was loved from the soul. He was telling me that everything was all right and that I had nothing to worry about. This is Ralph's natural manner, the way he behaves around everyone he meets. And it really moved me in an intimate and loving way.

At first, I was feeling shy and almost turned away from Ralph, but I stopped myself from any movement. I just forced myself to be physically still and to keep conversing. I noticed that Ralph was touching me, and this was when I started counting how many times! I could not easily touch him back (because of my early childhood programming), but I was completely comfortable with him.

He touched my shoulder for a moment, and then with a quizzical said, "I always touch people on the shoulder to give them a sense of well-being, that everything is all right. Most people are kind of skittish and nervous but calm down when I touch them like this. I worked with a lot of retarded persons at one point, and if I touched them like this, they would immediately relax and be loving."

And then he gazed at me with a strange, penetrating look. "But you behave differently," he said. "Most people immediately seem to relax and get in touch with their inner person when I touch them on the shoulder. In some way, you are already relaxed or you already have that connection I give people when I touch them."

I smiled at Ralph and laughed heartily. "Oh, when you are touching people on the shoulder you are giving them grounding," I explained. "I've studied energy work for many years. The first thing we always do is create grounding so that the body will feel safe and sound in any situation. Then we can bring in our higher nature or higher information."

"You do not need to be touched on the shoulder," he remarked.

"Yes," I agreed. "Most people are really insecure about their bodies, but I have grounding."

Ralph did not stop touching me. He just did not touch my shoulder. And I was happy that he kept touching me because, even though I was insecure with my body, this allowed me to love myself more. It had nothing to do with Ralph at all, but with me. Neither did it have anything to do with touching, but with the fact that we usually do not get enough validation early in life to love ourselves. Our parents love us, but often do not demonstrate this enough. So we grow up nervous about our bodies and our emotions until someone like Ralph comes along who can reach us—with either a physical touch or an emotional statement.

Releasing your insecurity has to do with more than physical touching, however. I have noticed that many young fathers are very involved with their babies. Everywhere, the younger generation of men are telling me that they never got enough love from their fathers and they don't want to do the same thing to their children. "We want to be real fathers. We want to experience our children and give this special time to them that we did not get." But more than time and love, they are giving permission for their young ones to be physically and emotionally secure. They are emotionally "touching" their children so they can be in touch with their soul nature. I feel we are at a very special juncture in history in which it is exciting to watch the beginning of an entirely different generation of more secure people.

CREATING SECURITY WITHIN YOURSELF

Often we act as if the world around us creates our reality and we just have to "put up" with this. But, as someone who is able to see how energy works, I have come to another conclusion. From a spiritual point of view, I believe *you create your own reality*. You can have the kind of life you want.

When you are insecure and try to overcontrol, however, the quality of life is immeasurably reduced. It does not take much time or energy to know inner security. If you consciously focus on releasing fears and old patterns, you can shift your entire life view. Discover the joy, the love and the success you were meant to have as you act out your desires through your passionate nature.

The following is a list of actions you can take to create more security in yourself:

Find your humor, which raises your physical, emotional, mental and spiritual energy. You can better see the irony in life and more easily follow your inner passion.

Forgive everyone for everything.

Practice the exercise in Appendix A for releasing fear.

Practice the exercise in Appendix A for acknowledging and letting go of insecurities.

Practice the exercise in Appendix A for dealing with concepts of perfection.

Practice the exercise in Appendix A for accessing the "I Am" state of being.

Every day, list five things about what a great person you are.

Learn to know and trust yourself and your decisions.

Learn to feed yourself your own loving nature.

Tell yourself, every day, that right now you are the very best of whatever you could be. Every day and in every way you are getting better and better.

Create five of your favorite positive inner statements (positive reinforcements), and say them to yourself whenever you feel any type of insecurity.

Make a list of your passionate soul desires, and strive to accomplish these every day in every way.

Praise yourself for every job well done and for everything you have tried to do, whether or not it seemed successful. Praise yourself for doing your best.

CHAPTER 7
Releasing Soul Conflict

Inner conflict often feels like a war is constantly going on inside. We all experience conflict caused by different desires happening simultaneously. This is the very nature of being in a human body that exists in time and space. Having a body means you will experience emotions, which means you will also experience conflict.

In fact, the system we use for socializing our children is a cause of conflict. As a child, you are hungry and want to grab the food with your hands, but you are taught to use a knife and fork. You are therefore socialized to eat with manners. Fore example, you must learn to wait—to say a prayer, to let everyone else sit down, or to have all of the main dishes be placed on the table. You are instructed to sublimate your desires, to resist your immediate passionate response, to act according to social standards set by your parents, your society and your tradition. You are trained to listen and obey the rules. We call this being human or civilized, or just "not acting like an animal." This training may be necessary, but so is understanding of the needs and wants of your physical vehicle.

After becoming fully socialized, we often lose the connection from body to soul that integrates our higher wisdom into active passions. We cannot connect with the feelings of the moment that make life special. So we lose the meaning of life. Once this meaning is lost, that fragile connection with the soul is often forgotten, or mythologized and no longer seen as an important part of the human condition.

When you act from your true soul nature, you easily find answers or methods of dealing with your conflicts. Likewise, whenever something does not work, you can shift the conflict and, instantaneously, your life will shift. This allows you to heal yourself, become more successful, have good relationships and experience your happy and joyous nature every day.

ARE YOU A SOUL IN CONFLICT?

If you recognize your conflicts, you can minimize or solve them. If you do not recognize them or just ignore them, you may get out of touch with your passionate soul. This creates stress and tension in your body. As you sabotage yourself in this way, you begin to feel cheated from not expressing your true desires.

Recognize conflicts within yourself

It is a beautiful day and you want to go to the beach, but you have to go to work.

You have to finish a project for work in the evening, but you want to go to a concert.

You promised to help you friend move, but really you feel like reading a book.

You want to go to the movie with your friend, but you have to finish a project for work.

You want to go to the party, but you promised your child you would take her to a movie.

You love two people and do not know whom to marry—you truly love both of them, but have to make a decision.

You are happily married, but you also love someone else.

You love your parents, but they irritate you and sometimes you hate what they do.

You like your business friend a great deal, but the offer his company made to your company is not acceptable and you cannot do business with him.

You love someone, but whenever you live with this person you have a miserable time in life.

It is a holiday and you have to travel to be with your family, but really you would just like to kick back, stay at home and just enjoy yourself.

Recognize conflicts with others

You want to go to a romantic movie, but your boyfriend/husband wants to go to a war movie.

You want to watch a ballgame on TV, but your girlfriend/wife wants to watch an old, romantic movie.

Your idea of fashion is very different from your parents. They do not want you to wear makeup, to get a tattoo or to pierce your body. They want you to wear a conservative hairstyle.

Your mother wants you to get married, but you want to travel and see the world first.

You want to visit your mother, but your wife is interested only in visiting *her* mother.

You do not want to take care of your mother-in-law. However, your husband believes that, even though she is senile and needs a great deal of constant help, his mother should remain in her home. You will have to stay home and care for her because your husband is always at work.

You work hard all day to pay for the support of your home and wife and children, and when you go home, you want to relax. But your wife wants you to help with the children and to take care of the house.

DO YOU SABOTAGE YOURSELF WITH 'HAVE TOS'?

Whenever you do not admit to the truth, you are sabotaging yourself. Sometimes, when you are at work or with relatives, you will agree to do something you do not like to do. You will smile and say all of the right things, acting as if you love to do this. But, in reality, you are either bored or cringing inside. Sometimes we do things just to please or help others, or to pay off debts. To keep the integrity of your passionate soul, however, you must consciously know and admit "to yourself" that you are doing this. If you try to make believe that you love doing something you hate, you will set up a lie within your own universe and eventually lose your self-integrity.

As a spiritual counselor, I see many young people who are miserable in marriages because they have lied to themselves. They told themselves that they love someone whom they do not love at all. They confused security with passion or sex with love. Always be honest with your own inner self by using your inner voice and speaking to your soul essence. This is your inner intuitive nature that always tells you what feels right. It is wise to cultivate this ability by taking the time to practice what you feel on a deeper level.

Sometimes people sabotage themselves with "have tos." They tell themselves they have to go to the concert or they have to baby sit for their cousin when they don't want to. They say they have to do special errands for their spouse. Or, they believe they have to send a Christmas card to everyone they know, or respond to everyone who sent one to them, when they really don't have the time or the inclination.

When you begin to experience a "have to," try to realize that you do not have to, but you *choose to.* Otherwise, you are acting under duress and without a sense of your free will. Perhaps you really do have to do something, either traditionally or socially. Maybe you have a real responsibility to your family. A good deal of the time, however, you can instead choose to do it because you "want to." You might even find then that you really enjoy doing it.

If you do feel that you have to do something and have no choice, be clear and wise enough to admit this to yourself. Allow yourself to enjoy the situation the most that you can, even though it is a "forced" one. You have the choice to create your life in a joyous happy manner, regardless of the circumstances. You don't have to suffer or sabotage your emotional life. It is up to you!

CAN YOU LIVE AND LET LIVE?

If you live intimately with another person (spouse, in-law, cousin), you may feel you have to bend yourself to fit in with someone else's rules and lifestyle. Some people call this compromise. Other people experience it as losing a part of their personality. For example, you may marry someone who does not eat mushrooms and so, for the rest of your married life, you do not eat mushrooms. I have had clients who change the type of soap they use, their toothpaste, their food habits, their clothing, their hairstyle, their sleeping habits and even their underwear to fit in with or please their partner.

Sometimes the most difficult thing about marrying is suddenly discovering that you always have to consider the wants and needs of the other person. Being married can include asking the other person's permission to do something, remembering to call home to check in, or caring enough to take care of the other person through the ups or downs of life together. Some people adjust easily to always being aware of another's needs, but there are those who feel restricted or restrained from expressing themselves spontaneously.

Do you have specific rules you expect the people around you to follow? Do you follow the lifestyle rules of a spouse, in-law, roommate, parent or intimate partner? Can you live with someone and still maintain your own original essence of personality? Often, the tensest situations after marriage are the lifestyle conflicts with in-laws in shared space or conforming to another family's style of food preparation or entertainment.

To coexist with relatives or in-laws, you need a sense of humor and the ability to live and let live. What do you insist upon having for your lifestyle that you will not change for anyone? What do you change to please others? What irritates you about the people you live with? Have you learned to release your irritation and sense of perfection?

ARE YOU HONEST WITH YOURSELF?

Many clients have been married for more than ten or twenty years and are not happy, but they do not have the courage to leave. What types of lies are you living? Are you honest with yourself? Lies sabotage the connection between your conscious mind and your passionate soul. I know two people who have the perfect marriage in public, but at home they never speak or interact. It is sad to see them purposely perpetuating a lie for their relatives, friends or company.

If you are living a lie, take a moment to do this little exercise. You may want to change your situation but feel it is impossible or not worth the effort or financial loss. In this exercise, you can see your life from another angle. Close your eyes and allow yourself to see yourself living your lie as you now exist. Now shift it and put your best friend in your situation and ask what she or he would do. Now shift again and put your favorite teacher in your situation. Shift again and put your mother or father in your situation. Then pick a well-known person whom you respect, put that person in your situation and see what that person would do.

When you finish looking, give yourself permission to forgive every person that you feel restricts you or causes you pain. Forgiveness releases your hold on things. It allows karma to be cleared, cuts energy that binds you and dissolves the anguish in your passionate soul. If you can forgive the other person and yourself, every situation can shift for the better.

BALANCING YOURSELF WHEN IN CONFLICT

Conflict is not necessarily something terrible, but a normal experience. We create conflict to learn how to balance our emotions. Everyone has some sort of conflict within. To eliminate conflict, some people go to temples or classes to learn to meditate. Others ignore their conflicts, but this practice will only hurt you. To truly deal with your conflict, you first have to admit to it. Then, you can release it using some of the skills in Appendix A.

You can also simply experience conflict without identifying with either side of your dilemma. I call this walking the tightrope. You can walk down the middle of conflict by admitting to yourself what is happening, but staying in the center point. If you do not identify with your two conflicting aspects, you will discover that you are not at war with yourself but simply an observer of your conflict phenomenon.

Another way to achieve balance when in conflict is to find the sweet "carrot" of life that helps you heal and be successful. My close friend Gretchen was having a conflict between what she felt and how she was acting. This can allow someone to stay ill, to feel bad and to lose faith in herself. In my friend's case, she almost let inner conflict control her life, until she found her "carrot."

A few months ago, Gretchen sent me a note by e-mail. She is a lovely, young European woman in her thirties who lives in California. When she was in her teens, she had the devastating experience of being diagnosed with cancer. She fought the cancer and won and has been healthy ever since then. But Gretchen remembered this as the most trying time of her life. If you have ever had a relative who has fought this deadly disease and won, you will know that it took every ounce of their focus and will power day after day. My friend remembered this period of her life with a bit of horror, wishing never to go through anything like it again.

When I received the e-mail from Gretchen, I was totally shocked. She had started a new job eight months before and often traveled to Europe. She loved her job because it allowed her to revisit many of her childhood haunts in Europe as well as meet new and interesting people. And so, I had thought she was very happy and well balanced. But her e-mail stated something completely different. Basically, Gretchen had been very sick for the last month.

She wrote, "I've not eaten well while traveling and am not taking care of myself. Symptoms similar to those in my teenage years have started to return. I feel a terrible malaise, as if I will die. My doctor thinks I might have some terrible genetic disease. If I do, this time I'll not fight it, but let it take its course."

To me, Gretchen's e-mail read like a suicide letter. She was one of the most positive people I had ever met, and this tone of not lifting a hand to fight her condition was most unexpected. I was in Tokyo at the time, and she was in California, so I immediately e-mailed her ex-husband, who lived in her area. He was still her close friend, a graduate of my clairvoyant school and a professional spiritual healer. I explained what she had written and asked him to please check in with her immediately.

Two days later, I received another e-mail from Gretchen. She had spent some time with her ex-husband, and he had done a marvelous clairvoyant reading for her. "He told me that my true soul mate, a very handsome man, would soon be coming into my personal universe. I have to get myself together for this. I will have to get some new makeup and fix my hair. I want to look good for this man should he really show up," she wrote.

It soon became obvious that Gretchen had switched her attention to the positive act of preparing to meet her soul mate instead of allowing herself to die. Almost instantaneously, she had switched from hopeless to hopeful.

Now, I did not know if what her ex-husband had said was true. But, more important, I knew he realized that Gretchen was caught in conflict. This "I want to get better, but I don't want to go through this fight again" attitude is common to many sick people. It is a losing of faith accompanied by fear of having to "fight" a disease full force every single, difficult, wearing day for months or years. Meanwhile, her ex-husband had used what we call the "carrot and stick" routine. He had put something out in front of her that would definitely give her the energy and faith to go forward, to step through the conflict and want to heal. In short, her desire for a soul mate was stronger than her fear of having to deal with the long process of fighting off a disease.

My friend's desire would actually cause her to heal quickly to have what she wanted. A week later, I received another e-mail from Gretchen. She was still happily preparing to meet her soul mate. The medical tests showed nothing alarming, even though the doctors did not understand her symptoms. Nevertheless, she was already feeling better and was assured she would heal herself.

We often become depressed and give up too easily. When you have a big conflict and feel low, look for the "carrot" in your life. This will give you permission to turn conflict around, to lift yourself past it. Sometimes you have to spark yourself so you can realign your universe with your true desires.

CHAPTER 8
Freeing Yourself – And Others Around You

Freedom is an illusive concept. Often you think you are free only to discover later that you were acting from your programming—what your mother or father wanted you to do. This is acceptable when you are twelve years old, but if you are age thirty or fifty and do this, you are losing your ability to create your own life.

Most of us carry a massive encyclopedia's worth of excess baggage, such as proper behavior, rules and regulations, duties and responsibilities. These are our dos and don'ts, goods and bads. You can release these alien programs of patterned behavior. When you give yourself permission to have the freedom of your inner soul, you also liberate the people around you to be their true selves.

DOING THE RIGHT THING

Who tells you what is the right to do? Who says what you are to be responsible for? Who decides how you should behave socially? Who tells you what is moral or immoral? Are you following the rules and regulations of your parents? From what source did your parents receive these rules?

We people of the United States are from many different backgrounds, so we have various cultural values. And now, we have to face new moral issues about the true responsibility of a citizen. Should we have a preemptive war? Is it right to invade another country to protect our own? When given orders in a military situation, should we question the morality of those orders? Should we object if we are told to do something that is not in good conscience? What once was understood and agreed to by everyone might now be questionable and might be decided by each and every one of us singly.

As we move into the new millennium with its constantly shifting financial situations and radical social concepts, what was once totally accepted as part of the culture is now in great flux. For instance, in Japan there is more personal crime, some of which is absolutely heinous. In the traditional past, this type of behavior was an extreme exception because all actions reflected profoundly upon one's entire family.

And so, the human race is moving into adulthood as it evolves on a social and moral level. This means that instead of being followers—being told what to do and what is right and wrong—we are learning to be personal decision makers. Each of us is slowly, yet certainly, becoming a leader from the inside out. But, what must we do to be in the purity of our own spirit? I believe that simply being in touch with your passionate nature puts you closer to the Buddha-like nature of universal awareness. It is the active Christ force and Goddess compassion nature that heals people and brings them to their own inner peace.

Now I know that my words may seem like a total paradox. I am saying that being in touch with your passionate nature allows you to find not just passion, but universal awareness in the form of inner peace and the oneness that heals. We have been taught that passions cause us to act out our desires. Nevertheless, if your passions are true and totally what you are meant to do, then you will act out the scenario of returning to inner peace, the Source within. Your passions were created by God to spur you on. They are the true expression of your soul acting out your life purpose through your body.

When you are truly in touch with your life purpose, you always act out of your highest nature. Therefore, your passionate soul is not just about following your desires, but actually acting out the nature of what you agreed to do before taking your present body. It is what you incarnated to manifest. When you do this, you are on-line. Thus, everything you do is with purpose and intention as planned by your Higher Self.

SHOWING FORGIVENESS

When someone restricts your freedom, you will probably react with anger. This might be the anger of a five-year-old who is not allowed to run across the street, or it might be the anger of a young adult who has been programmed to marry the wrong type of person for lasting happiness. But your parents were probably seeking to keep their child safe from traffic when they set up such restrictions. That is, parents usually mean well and act out of love. Likewise, parents who instill a need in their child to marry the wrong type of mate most likely are loving and mean well, even if the results are devastating in the child's life. Nonetheless, the truth is that someone cannot truly let go of an old program until the programmer is forgiven.

Forgiveness is the act of release, of letting go of conflict generated from all artificial commands, even if lovingly placed or on an unconscious level. Letting go of a controlling program is returning the command back to the command center. By giving the program back to the programmer, you allow him to stop taking responsibility for you. The programmer must now deal entirely with his own actions, taking responsibility for his own actions instead of trying to take responsibility for you.

In grammar school, I had a friend who lived on my block. She and I were firm and fast best friends, telling one another all of our private thoughts and feelings. One day, a new girl moved to our town and joined our class. My best friend liked her and started spending time with her. Soon, she was telling her my personal feelings about things, things I had told my friend in confidence. When I walked past the two of them in the hallways, they would point at me, make nasty comments and laugh. I was very hurt and simply ignored both of them from that time on.

In my own way, I hardened my heart and acted as if my friend did not exist. A year later, her new friend moved away; she was alone and approached me to be her friend. I never answered her, but just ignored her as if she did not exist. I ignored her for three full years. I knew that after a year I should have simply let it all go, but instead I made a point of being angry and steeling myself to look the other way. It took a lot of energy to ignore her while I would revisit all of my feelings of being abused. And each time I saw her, I would feel tense and stiff.

Finally, when I had a new friend and felt secure within myself, my old friend and I were placed on the same gym team. Somehow, I could allow myself to forgive her. I never became friendly with her again, but we could talk comfortably about nonpersonal subjects. I began to notice that whenever I saw her, my body did not tense anymore. After forgiving her, I would feel nothing emotional at all when she passed by. I had in some way released all of my anger, spitefulness, hurt and tension. If I could have understood this earlier, I'd have forgiven her a lot sooner.

I had learned that whatever you feel for another person is what you carry within yourself, and it can actually hurt you more than the other person. Forgiveness is the skill of releasing the past and enjoying the present. To forgive also creates instant healing in families—situations between mothers or fathers and their children or between relatives. You can clean up past karmic debts so you do not carry forward any burden.

Returning lost or unwanted energy

When someone is controlling you (consciously or unconsciously), you can have underlying anger. You may not be aware of it, but this person has encroached on your free will. Even if you are not aware, you may act out of anger when you are near that person. Once you realize that you are being controlled by someone else's program, you can simply recognize it and return it. The act of giving it back can afford a tremendous sense of freedom. You will never be at its mercy again.

To return a program, energetically imagine taking the words, images, feelings or whatever it seems to be and hand this back to the person who gave it to you. Of course, you will be responding energetically and do not have to tell the person verbally that you found their program. It is wise also to thank the person nonverbally for his or her kind wishes, saying that you no longer need this help.

When individuals give you a program or a belief system, they are handing you some of their energy. This is their life force and not a good thing to give away. By returning this life force, you also give them better health and more energy throughout their day. Then you are acting as your own adult and taking responsibility for your actions. Thus, you can relate to the other person from a position of personal power. You are now discovering what impassions you to act and deciding what to create.

This handing-back process seems very useful to many individuals in their twenties, for example. After giving back programs to their parents, they often enjoy a much better relationship.

Returning someone else's program is therefore the act of defining your own reality. As a grown-up, it is the first act of responsibility you will own, one that separates you energetically from your parents. Some people take this act of self-definition only after their parents die. By that time, though, you have usually made many life decisions based on someone else's needs and values. This can lead to a great deal of unresolved inner conflict because you have not acted out of your own passions. But each time you listen to your inner voice instead, belief in yourself is reinforced.

Releasing what does not belong to you

Without restrictions, you can be a new person. Restrictions may be one of two things. First, they may be your own belief system that does not allow you to do something. This is your own moral or internal set of values that will not give you permission. You may believe that it is "wrong," or that you do not "deserve" something or that it is not the "right thing to do" at that time. I have noticed that many of my friends restrict their ability to have things. I call this low self-esteem or restrictions that create lack of abundance. Although everyone has some of these, some people have a lot of self-imposed restrictions.

It is wise to pay attention to your inner voice if it says you cannot do something until you finish something else, or until you "deserve" it. You might want to release such words or put more positive concepts on your inner tape if you hear the following scenarios:

> "I do not deserve to have this."
> "I cannot have this until, for example,
>> my children grow up and go to college.
>> my children go to school
>> I graduate from college and get a good job
>> I get married
>> I make a certain amount of money
>> I get a better position at work
>> I feel better about myself.

When you release inner restrictions of this kind, you can have more freedom to do things and still be a good person.

Other people's beliefs or programs that are in your personal universe can lead to restrictions. You do not want someone else's belief system no matter who they are. When you free yourself from parental programming, for instance, you also free your parents from responsibility on a karmic level. You have your own body so you can experiment and learn from being yourself. You are here to learn free will, the act of making your own decisions. You might remove your parents' marriage programming and still go on to marry exactly the type of person they wanted you to marry. This, however, is your choice, not someone else's. It becomes your learning experience, and that's what life is all about. Plus, everyone gains more freedom in this type of win-win situation.

REDEFINING YOUR SENSE OF SELF

Each of us is made up of many aspects of personality held together by the common threads of body type, cultural identity and common beliefs. Whenever you shift or change any of these beliefs or concepts, your entire identity has to shift as well. This is why most people prefer to remain entrenched in their negative or stuck patterns rather than take the risk to change. But if you do not shift, you may remain mired in your own garbage. So don't box yourself in by always having to know who you are. Just allow yourself to be.

When you get up in the morning, who are you? Do you have an identity at breakfast? What is your identity on your way to work? Who are you when you get to work? If you go out to lunch with a friend, who do you become? If you go to aerobics class or the gym after work, who are you? And when you return home, are you the same person?

Finding your true self can be an art form. You have more control over your life if you consciously choose who you are and shift different aspects of yourself at will. This allows you the freedom to experiment with your actions and emotions as well.

See if you can list every aspect that you are: mother/father; daughter/son; aunt/uncle; your job title; your favorite sport; your hobby or interests; your emotions and so on. Here's an example: Janet Ayerson— Christian, resident of Los Angeles, mother, daughter, aunt, nurse, golfer, pottery artist, calligrapher, knitter, exuberant, shy, middle aged (30s), soft spoken, ecologist, loves animals, ballroom dancer, loves romantic movies and books, adores key lime pie.

Now put these aspects in order of most used, so that the top of your list is the aspect you find yourself being the most. Notice, however, how you are many aspects at the same time. Also, observe that you are not listing certain aspects even though they are also a part of you. As you experience transformational change, new aspects of yourself may appear, including some you do not know, do not like or do not understand. To accept this, you will probably need to rearrange your entire inner reality, unless you learn to innately accept yourself in whatever way you happen to be.

So, if our example, Janet, has an argument with her daughter and feels that she has been cruel or callous as a mother, Janet will have to absorb the consequences of her actions and see herself in an aspect that she does not like. If she suddenly goes to a neighborhood ecology meeting and finds herself speaking and organizing, she will notice that she is not always a shy person, but sometimes an active, verbal, aggressive, outgoing person. This recognition will surely change her self-image.

The best way to redefine your sense of self is to BE all of your aspects just as they happen for you. If you always see yourself in one particular way, however, you may have difficulty adjusting to your new self when you change, as we all do. When you are accepting of yourself, you will not only be able to change easily, but also like yourself more. Further, you will give yourself more. Your ability to have material items, emotional growth and love will also increase. When you accept yourself, you give love to yourself. This allows you to have more of everything.

When you look at your aspects, be sure to check out which of these are truly yours. Sometimes we incorporate aspects of our mother and father that are destructive to us. If your mother is anxiety prone or your father is judgmental, you do not have to incorporate this behavior. You can love your parents and still not aspire to be exactly like them. If you find aspects of yourself that mirror qualities of your parents or teachers, use the releasing exercises in Appendix A. Finding yourself is allowing yourself to be entirely you.

DEALING WITH INVALIDATION

When you say or do something that threatens other people, they may react by invalidating your ability to exist. Threatened people do this by sending out some hurtful energy that says you are not okay. Once you are invalidated, your energy often falls, your self-esteem sinks and you feel less enthusiastic about your project or yourself. Inversely, people tend to validate you whenever you do something that supports their lifestyle or belief system.

I had a friend in San Francisco who used to get all sorts of exciting, creative ideas about how to start a small business. One day she would want to start an import-export business, and the next she was interested in selling her handcrafted small purses, vests and shirts to a local boutique. Every time we met, my enthusiastic friend would inform me of a new moneymaking idea.

One day, I asked why she had not instituted any of these hot, entrepreneurial ideas. She told me that a "family advisor" had said they wouldn't work. Well, my friend had a sister who was a little jealous and a lot threatened by her super creative ideas. When she would pass these ideas by her sister, this "family advisor" would invalidate everything. Over a period of time, my friend had never really created anything. I taught her how to take her sister's invalidation and release it from her personal universe. Today she has both a shop stocked full of imports and a business that provides handmade clothing to local boutiques. She is doing well financially and, more important, she has learned to listen to her own information, releasing any invalidation that comes her way.

Sometimes people invalidate you because they feel they could not do the same thing you want to do. And often this energy comes in a hidden way. The mother of one of my friends seemed entirely supportive of everything she did, telling her that she could be successful in whatever she wanted to do. But one day, my friend noticed that any idea she told her mother would fizzle out and simply not work. So she tried my skill for removing invalidation and soon realized that what her mother *said* and what her mother *did* were two entirely different things.

Her mother would say very positive things, but at the same time she felt a negative undercurrent. Her mother was from the generation of women who were not allowed to accomplish things out in the world. Although she mentally supported her daughter, the mother's inner emotional outlook was broadcasting that this was not possible. Hence, everything the daughter mentioned about worldly ideas was buried under the mother's invalidation. Once her daughter refused to accept this invalidation, her ideas were successful. The relationship with her mother also seemed to improve.

If you feel that you get easily invalidated, check Appendix A for how to release invalidation. Learn also how to not accept it in the first place.

LOVING YOURSELF

I have found that the more love you give to yourself, the more love you can give to others. And, when you give more to yourself, you can have more success, better relationships, improved health and finer self-esteem. When you act out of your true passions, you have no reason to criticize, invalidate or conflict yourself.

It is easy to say, "Just love yourself." But how can we do this? First, get rid of whatever does not allow you to love yourself, such as invalidation, self-criticism, fear and a simple lack of permission. Begin to release these negative concepts by putting them in a box and blowing them up. This easy, yet powerful skill is presented in Appendix A. Second, once you begin to release your negatives, you will want to refill your personal universe with positives.

There are also some primary skills for bringing love into your life. For example, you can give yourself permission to be a loving person. That is, practice self-love and spread that love to your family, friends and work companions. Use the permission gauge in Appendix A. If you have a low permission rating for self-love, then raise it by 5 percent every day until it is much higher.

You can fill up the empty spaces in yourself with love by using the energetic technique of bringing in what clairvoyants call cosmic or universal love. Usually, this is a pink, peach or rose energy that fills up your body as if it were an empty balloon. If you do this several times a day, you will notice a difference in how you experience yourself. Your self-esteem will rise and you will feel comfortable from the inside out.

I had a client in Los Angeles who lost her husband to cancer. They had lived together for many years, and she soon sank into a state of depression and confusion about the meaning of life without him. Whenever someone close to you dies, you will experience a series of emotions passing through. If you admit to these feelings, you can stay in contact with your passionate self and eventually emerge from your grief intact as a human being. However, refusing to face the immediate reality of death, most people diverge into guilt. They may carry their grief for years to come instead of allowing themselves to process it out.

After losing a loved one, you will likely feel a range of emotions, including grief, anger, a sense of loss or emptiness, lack of self-worth or meaning in life, guilt, depression, despondency and eventually acceptance. Your initial grief might shift into anger at the person for leaving you. You may feel that nothing matters anymore, not even having money and possessions because they cannot bring someone back. Or you may feel guilty that you did not complete something or did not do more when your dear one was alive.

If you allow yourself to grieve and admit your true feelings, you can slowly work through the entire grieving process. It usually takes about a year. Eventually, you can accept the loss, still experience love for the departed person and also love yourself. If you stay stuck in any part of this process, such as still feeling anger, guilt or regret, then your inner conflict will not allow you to feel love for yourself. This condition does not give you permission to be alive now, so your life force and will to enjoy yourself will be diminished. Being true to your inner passionate soul allows you to move through grief and into the natural state of human awareness, namely the constant love of life.

When my client came in grief, confusion and despair, I forced her to face her feelings and to admit to everything she was feeling. Of course, I presented energetic skills for releasing her emotions, and I also explained that this experience couldn't be rushed. A year later when she visited our healing clinic, the change in her was dramatic and beautiful. She had emerged from her cocoon of loss and was in a state of love and acceptance. She had accepted her grief and transformed her experience into a positive state instead of a permanent loss. She glowed with the love of her inner self and did not need to be helped by the student healers who were attending. And yes, she still missed her husband, but she also acknowledged her right to life. She had connected with her inner passionate soul.

ENJOYMENT IS LIKE A RIPPLE IN A POND

When you act out of your true nature, the honest expression of who you are, you allow yourself to enjoy life to its fullest. People who do this seem to radiate or glow. They are connected. When you see them, you feel that they are the dynamic people, those who stand out in a positive way. They are like beacons of light showing the path to everyone else. It doesn't take courage to be your own person, but it takes some self-searching and inner fortitude. Thus, you are not only giving to yourself but also to everyone else around you. You are like a small stone thrown into the water whose ripples affect the entire pond as they spread outward.

When you are true to your own conscience, you also allow everyone else to have the same freedom! You become like the Statue of Liberty with one arm up holding a torch to light the path for others. The only difference is that you do not have to wear any special robes or stand out from others. You have to do only one thing—*you have to be you*. Yes, you have to totally and completely commit to your true inner self.

Perhaps this is living up to the ideals of courage, selflessness, sacrifice for others and honesty. Sometimes people forget that such attributes exemplify the concept of acting out of your passionate soul. But your true self is in alignment with what you came here to do as a spiritual being. You are walking your true path, which is not selfish or self-centered. When you walk the path you chose before incarnating, everything you do comes out of the God Force within.

You may think that you are not a special person or a dynamic person. You may believe you cannot live up to the ideals of your highest nature, which is often like the ancient Knight's or Lady's code of honor. You may feel you are just a common mortal, seeking to make life easier or more comfortable and workable for the moment. When you get in touch with your own passionate nature, however, you are living up to the highest ideals that exist on this planet. You become the expression incarnate of the best of the warriors and the best of God. You are exhibiting the truth of action and are purely what you were meant to be.

True enjoyment of yourself is doing what is right for both you and everyone else. It is living life to the fullest. When you rid yourself of restrictions, programs and beliefs set by others and get in touch with your true inner feelings, you will find that life is not fear and pain, but love and enjoyment. You might find that life is truly worth living.

Chapter 9
Expressing Your Passionate Sexual Nature

You can create permission to connect with your passionate sexual nature, which is an expression of your body. This is what energy practitioners and martial artists call your natural *chi*. In the process, you will awaken your body personality in this life and your passionate soul nature. When you go on-line with your sexuality, you also get in touch with what you came here to do.

If you have had any past experience that connects your sexuality with fear, however, you will have an instant inner program that can restrict both your relationships and your ability to be in touch with your sexuality. Fear twists and warps the inner core of your loving, sexual nature. The distorted energy of fear can emphasize the need for either the control or the over expression of sexual desires. This chapter suggests how sexual obsessions and dysfunction can be released if you can identify the fear.

THE SHADOW SIDE OF SEXUALITY

I have never truly understood why sexuality is one topic many people feel they are not allowed to discuss openly. Moreover, it is always targeted as the underlying bastion of immorality. Even though young persons in modern society often dress in a more sexual fashion than they did fifty years ago and feel they are more sexually liberated than their parents, we still find it largely taboo to speak honestly about sex. In public, most of us are not comfortable with sexual discussions, which easily disintegrate into crude jokes or gestures.

We should be comfortable with our bodies. As we get older, however, we tend to use our bodies less and to concentrate more on the mental aspects of work. Instead of being athletically active, we become passive participants who simply observe active people. We also have a tendency to move toward our spiritual essence instead of more knowledge of the body.

As a result, sexuality is often covered up and relegated to a secondary aspect of personality expression. This deemphasizing process discourages the expression of one's inner passions, restricting average adults from using their sensual nature as part of their loving personality with family, friends and coworkers. This denial causes internal conflict, which eventually freezes a person's sexuality both in and out of the bedroom, causing unnatural responses in general. Consequently, love and sex get separated when, for example, someone has proper or permissible sex with a spouse while looking for extracurricular partners with whom to have forbidden or racy sex.

The denial of loving, natural sexuality also causes people to hold needs and wants tightly within, and then to have a very difficult time expressing their feelings. This in turn promotes the perfunctory coming together of partners rather than their passionate, loving sexuality. Meanwhile, commercial interests increasingly pander to our sexual level of awareness. Magazine ads include hidden sexual symbols, adult comic books reveal extreme sexuality, automobiles are likened to desirable consorts and prominent clothing, lingerie and perfume ads sell more sensuality than products.

This shadow side of sexuality exists as a hidden part of mainstream culture. We are forbidden to mix countless needs and desires with "proper" interactions during the daylight hours. Instead, these feelings appear every evening at bars and private clubs and in erotic bookshops, films and literature. This shadow sexuality creates a double standard between what is allowed and spoken about in public compared to what is hidden from view, but acceptable to many.

The shadow content also causes people to say one thing, but to do another. For example, it propagates "love motels," but does not encourage spouses to return home and enjoy love for lunch. And, we have teenagers who feel free to have sex with adults for money, even though the general belief system regards this as immoral. Further, this shadow behavior cuts off the discussion of sex from one generation to another. As each new generation resets it own values, it usually rebels from the mores of the one before.

Clearly, we humans fear our own passions and our own bodies more than we love one another. If we were to release our fear, we could access these passions and be more open and loving. Even so, certain societal taboos are disappearing in America with the coming of AIDS and the resulting TV ads that get to the point about sexual arousal and protection. Ads of this nature would have been impossible a mere twenty-five years ago. Nevertheless, an open moral stance by the public is never guaranteed because, as time passes and new generations appear, we could well swing back to more secretive opinions about sexuality.

To bring the topic of sexuality back into the light, we need to combine sex, love, passion and family values in one big package, instead of compartmentalizing them. We must create a vision of what we want our society to be and then decide how to get it. But, historically, we just watch our teenage children go into hormonal overdrive and shake our heads in disapproval or disdain. But, we need to take charge of what we want. If we could understand ourselves as sensual, sexually expressive beings, such extremes between the activities of the day and the night would disappear. The people in suits would be more sensual and sexual within themselves and blatant, outrageous sexual expression would be history. In this way, we could attain a more balanced, natural sexual expression, which is truly the evolution of the human race.

ARE YOU FILLED WITH PROGRAMMING AND FEAR?

Take a moment to recognize when and how you express your sexual or sensual nature. At what time or during which situations do you have permission to express your passionate self? When do you not have permission to express this through your body movements, your actions or your dress?

Sometimes we fear our own desires, feeling that we might be obsessed with them. So we tune out every passionate response because we are afraid that we cannot control it. I hope to show that you can experience your passions without going off the deep end. People often have moral fears about expressing themselves. Being passionate, however, is not necessarily running off with your best friend's wife or husband! Instead, you will be more in touch with your own inner self and find ways to express whatever energizes you.

In 1989, I had a client who called for a clairvoyant reading by phone. She was in her early thirties and was about ninety pounds overweight. She asked what was causing her to gain so much weight. Sometimes being clairvoyant is like being a therapist who has the answers. That is, I can usually see what has been happening. But it is often wiser to *help people get their own answers*. Just giving the answers may seem too easy, and many people will not listen or truly understand. So, I asked this woman some questions.

"Have you always been overweight?"

"Oh, no!" she answered. "It all started when I was fourteen."

"What else happened when you were fourteen?" I prompted.

"I started to date," she said thoughtfully. "From that time until now, I repeatedly gained up to one hundred and twenty pounds, then I'd diet and take it off and then I'd put it back on again."

"How do you lose the weight?" I asked, very curious.

"Oh, I try everything," she admitted. "And it all works. Last time I used Slimfast and a doctor helped me."

"Was that recently?" I wondered.

"Yes. And I lost all of the weight. It was so simple and worked wonderfully."

"And then what happened?" I prodded her along.

"I gained it back."

"Just like that? Why did you gain it back?" I asked.

"It happened when I was in the shower one day," she continued. "I looked down at my body, and I became afraid. I mean, I was like a perfect size four and just so beautiful. But I felt that all these men would hit on me and look at me and make me feel ashamed. So I got afraid, and after that I ate as much as I could."

This conversation was truly wonderful because my client had spoken out about her own fear. It was much better than having me tell her that she feared men and her own passionate nature; that the childhood programming by her father to hide her sexuality and be ashamed of it had triggered her to eat when she was really not hungry at all. After that, it was easy to explain how to release the fear. I could show her how to allow herself to recognize and respond to her passionate feelings, how to have feelings of love and self-esteem for her body—thin or heavy—and how to recognize and release the emotional and moral programming of her father.

Then I helped her release as much programming as she was energetically ready let go of. I was hoping that, with knowledge and skills, she would soon be able to enjoy her beautiful body without having to play the yo-yo weight game. After releasing the fear, she could go on to use her passionate nature in a healthy fun manner and totally expand her love of life.

RECOGNIZING YOUR SEXUAL PROGRAMMING

A man came into my office for a clairvoyant reading. He was handsome, tall and probably in his mid-thirties. I sat across from him and closed my eyes, went into a light trance and scanned the screen in my mind's eye to see whatever I would see.

I saw him looking at beautiful women. He would look at them, become enamored with their glamour and want them. Then, once he got someone, he would find that they had nothing in common. He seemed to be seeing women only from the outside. For example, he saw their physical beauty but did not connect with their personality or inner essence. He also seemed out of touch with his own inner passion, which was probably why he desired beautiful women in the first place. But, he could not act appropriately once someone was there for him.

"You have the wrong taste with women!" I told him. "You marry for the wrong reasons."

He proceeded to tell me how right I was. He had been married five times and each relationship had soured right after the honeymoon. So I explained how to look for both inner and outer beauty in a woman, how to recognize one's own lasting passionate nature and how to take the time to make a satisfying choice. I never saw this client again, but I hope his sixth marriage is a truly passionate and lasting one.

Many men have programming that tells them women are not partners in the sexual act, but objects with which to satisfy their desires, someone they "do it to." This idea also leads to marriages with little intimate or deep communication, in which the man feels he always has to be in charge of the sexual act instead of engaging in a true sharing of passion.

Likewise, many women have had no permission from their parents to have sexual feelings. As they encounter sexuality or get married, they discover they do not "feel" fully or have trouble having orgasms. Often women do not speak about this and go for years in miserable marriages, submitting to sex instead of desiring it because they feel nothing from the experience. As a woman, you can remove your programming and train your mind and your feelings to accept sex as natural, pleasurable and loving.

Moral programs that disallow your passion have usually been put in place by parents, relatives, spiritual leaders and teachers. For example, young women are taught to sit with their legs closed. And men are taught a double standard that says they can release their desires with "certain types of women," but with "good girls," they must be restrained or civilized. I call this the day and night standard. Often you can actually hear your parents or teachers saying controlling phrases in your head!

Those who have given you a sexual program probably meant well. They are usually the adults in your life who wanted to help you, to give you guidelines. Instead, they really gave you their rules, which often become restrictions. Your own rules will work better for you than any others. This gives you freedom of expression and direct contact with your own body.

RELEASING YOUR SEXUAL FEARS

Everyone has sexual fears. Some people fear the power of their own sexuality, and others fear not being adequate or being rejected. Some people have performance fears, and others simply fear feeling so much at one time. If you are not consciously connected with your fears, you will deny these feelings. But they will always be there, right under the surface.

Sexual fears carry a great deal of energy because they are so taboo. They certainly are not thought of as normal dinner table conversation! Whenever you feel nervous or insecure in a sexual situation, you are encountering your fears. Whenever you reach for a drink or a cigarette or display nervous body mannerisms, you are facing your fears.

So, when you have these fears, you will need to release them constantly and consistently. As you watch yourself, you will be able to see your hidden fears. When this happens, train yourself to use the skill of putting them into a box and blowing them up (see Appendix A). If you do this often enough, you will begin to release the energy in them and they will disappear.

You can also send old sexual programs into the ocean. Just imagine them flowing down your legs, into the ground and through the water of the earth, which flows to the ocean. They thus return to the sea of life and are released. A more direct way is to take the program and give it back to the person who gave it to you. Simply giving someone's energy back is like giving them an energy healing.

When fear and programming lose their energy, you will feel much different inside. More at peace and naturally connected with your sensual, sexual side, you will be on the road to the true freedom of the passionate soul.

Assessing your sexual self

Before you can express your sexuality, you need to understand your sexual nature. What turns you on? When are you feeling something sexual or sensual? Do you allow yourself to feel your sexual feelings? Or do you immediately put a damper on them or try to ignore them? Do you try to hide your sexual nature? What kind of permission do you have to be sexual?

Sexuality is a natural part of our physical world, but most people are not totally comfortable with or they feel guilty about their sexuality. They are uncomfortable with both their body and their passionate soul.

If this has happened to you, there is something you can do to integrate this fascinating level of awareness into daily life.

Sensuality and sexuality are natural body expressions, part of a healthy personality. What does it mean to express your sexuality? Will you look or act in a different way at work? Consider what it is you experience when you feel sensual. Do you move your body differently?

I often use the following exercise in workshops for self-discovery. Find a medium-size room to walk in or an open place where people will not be watching. Now, just walk around in a circle, or simply walk for a short period of time. Walk the way you feel right now. Do you know what that is? If not, try to get in touch with what you feel inside, and express that with the way you walk. Now shift, walking as your sensual self.

In workshops, we over exaggerate this at first and then tone it down, expressing sensuality in a natural manner. Now shift again, and walk as your sexual self. What do you feel in your body when being your sexual self? What part of your body do you become aware of? How have you changed?

You are the same person, but your sensitivity to everything around you and to your body is different. Your sensitivity to people is different. Are you comfortable with this? If not, why? Do you have any negatives or fears that come up? Has anyone ever told you that it is wrong or bad to be sexual or sensual? Have they suggested it or implied it instead of directly telling you that?

Now walk as you would at work, and observe the energy or image aspect you express there. Does it have any of your sensuality or sexuality in it, or are you only a walking-talking head? In which of these ways are you most comfortable with your body? When you look at your friends, are they comfortable with their sensuality, their sexuality and their bodies? What kind of permission level do they give to you? Take your time to look at this information about your true self. Do you think you could express your sexuality or sensuality as a natural part of yourself at work or with friends? If not, why?

EXPRESSING YOUR SEXUAL SELF NATURALLY

Your sensuality and sexuality are entwined with the inner core of your body. Although being sexual at work does not necessarily mean *acting* in a different way, it certainly is about *feeling* different. When you are in alignment and feel in touch with your *inner* self, you feel comfortable with who you are and what you do.

Many people get confused about how to express their sexuality. They think that wearing certain clothes, putting on a type of makeup, walking in a particular manner or dying their hair a different color makes them sexual. But nothing outside of you can make you sexual or sensual. These are simply external things that people use to express themselves, to conform to others around them or to fit into a particular image.

In the last half-century, people have learned to use exotic externals to make statements about their unique personality or their ability to be creative. It does take some talent to create an image, but it takes more knowing how to initiate new forms instead of just seeing yourself through someone else's eyes. Nonetheless, young people often try to outdo one another by adopting the latest dress or hair fashion craze. But this limited creativity only mirrors or reworks ideas. Creativity of the soul will bring you to entirely new ways of expressing your inner self, which is fosters the evolution of the human race.

Sexuality is a natural sense and involves the act of moving, speaking, feeling and seeing. You *are* naturally sensual, and clothing merely accents or expresses who *you* are from within. The feeling of sensuality can thus be expressed no matter what you wear or where you are. Only you can give yourself permission to act and feel sensual. If you rely on external, societal rules or permission from other people, you will always feel stifled and separated from your passionate self. Remember that the people who "give" permission can also always "take" it away. So, set your own personal guidelines and be in charge of your own morality.

Sexuality is thus a connection with your passions and your body, with your soul and your physical essence. Once you are in touch with your natural sensuality, you will be comfortable with your sexuality and feel energized. This energy is the life force of your soul expressing itself through your body.

Chapter 10
Passionate Spirituality, Language of the Soul

A soul is the higher nature of a human being. It is the lasting, immortal part of you that moves from life to life. Therefore, the soul has access to the oneness of the God nature and the higher information level of the universe.

You soul is a living spiritual entity. You are energy that never dies, but simply transforms as it grows. Your soul is life force that creates and uses your human body to learn and grow. And, in turn, you can access your soul to get a better job, find your life mate, have a better relationship with a lover or your family, create better health or generally have a more fulfilling life, according to your true destiny.

What is your soul nature?

For centuries, metaphysicians and healers have discussed, debated and written about the existence of the soul. Not everyone is immediately interested in this topic, but it can help us understand the connection with our true energy source. Rather than recount the many arguments about the nature of the soul, I will give just my personal opinion of what a soul connection is really all about.

Your soul reincarnates from life to life on the wheel of destiny, seeking to learn and complete its tasks and agreements. Very few people realize that humanity is a conglomeration of building blocks from many lifetimes, organized like the chapters of an unfinished book. If you are Buddhist, Shinto, Hindu or Pagan, perhaps you have been introduced to this concept through religious texts or statements made by your parents. Or, you may have read books mentioning your karma and dharma, or heard traditional religious stories when you were a child. The Catholic Church outlawed the idea of reincarnation in the third century so most Christians do not consciously have this belief. Before this time, however, most people in the ancient world were familiar with the cycle of rebirth.

The soul connection to your body is an ultimate, radiant energy source. This part of you is the real you—the energy that fuels your body, the spark of illumination that lights your mind to action and the will to explore your emotional nature, which is available only through the body. This is also your direct connection to the God Source, or the life source of the universe.

Separate from the soul is your energy self, or what some metaphysicians call the Higher Self. This pure energy part of you has a separate identity. When you get in touch with your Higher Self, you gain the knowledge of who you truly are. You discover your true life path, how to know and remember past lives and how to get high-level information that will make your life easier. Becoming aware in this way also enables you to make the total direct connection to your passionate soul. Once connected, you have a direct line from the essence of universal energy to your emotional center.

It is difficult to function at your highest potential when you are out of touch with your passionate soul. Losing your passionate soul is not just being bored, deadened and out of touch with your life. It can also actually be losing the very precious connection with your soul essence, the part of you that aligns you with universal life force. Thus, losing touch can be the cause of sickness, disease, loss of the will to live and inability to communicate well with the people around you.

There are different theories about what the soul is and where it is connected into the body. Often people confuse the Higher Self with the soul, but they are actually two different energy essences. The soul is considered to be the spiritual and immortal part of humans, the ennobling part of human nature. It is seen as the seat of perception and activity in humans. This belief in the soul as immortal is common to most religions, philosophies and spiritual belief systems throughout the world. However, opinions about the character, origin and actions of the soul vary greatly.

In the Western world, the Greek philosopher Plato believed that the soul pre-exists the body and that it is immortal. Another Greek philosopher, Aristotle, believed that the soul forms the material that makes the body into a human being and that the soul is immortal. He suggested, however, that the soul survives the body by preserving the mind to go on to immortal depths. Later, Thomas Aquinas, a Christian religious figure, followed Aristotle's thoughts and suggested that the soul is immortal, spiritual, intellectual and a part of the human body. He believed that the soul is created at some definite moment in the formation of the human body, but he was unclear about when this occurs. These philosophers set forth beliefs that have influenced religious thought through the ages— from the Christian Church and the Western world's belief systems to the present day. Most Christians now believe in life after death, although the Bible does not provide a clear description of how a person survives after loss of the physical body.

In Hindu thought, the soul, or atman as it is called, is seen as being identical with the world soul or Brahman. Hindus perceive the atman as passing from one incarnation to the next. To a Hindu believer, salvation is the cessation of the act of passing through incarnations, the end of the cycle of reincarnation. The attainment of realizing freedom from the necessity of more incarnations is called nirvana.

In Buddhism, however, there is no sense of a surviving self, such as the atman. Meditation leads to the awareness that the idea of self or atman is an illusion. Buddhism is said to have the concept of reincarnation, but it doesn't usually regard something as passing from one body to the next.

From a metaphysical and clairvoyant point of view, the Higher Self is your energy self divided into three distinct parts:

1. The highest part is the purely spiritual part that connects with religion, archetypes and your higher nature. Most of the time, we do not pay much conscious attention to it. This part of your higher nature connects with your Buddha nature, the Zen of your spiritual quest, the ability to search for and find the true Holy Grail, the ability and need to channel and become one with the divine archetypes people call Gods and Goddesses and the infinite, unconditional loving nature of divine spirit that says we are all always a part of the whole.

2. The middle part bridges your higher God-like self and your lower "needs and wants" body personality. Usually, this middle part is what clairvoyants call the higher mind. This energy introduces ideas to you that become new inventions, philosophies or musings on the physics of the natural world. It is your higher mind that lends itself to discoveries about improving humankind and making a better world. Plato, Aristotle, Plotinus, Shotoko Taishi, Kitaro Nishida, Einstein and John Lennon were people who were hooked into the higher mind and so benefited humankind.

3. The lowest part generally takes care of your body. This is the part of you that makes basic decisions about whom you will marry, what job you will take, which route you will take home and how to deal with basic day-to-day problems. It is third and lowest part that learns the most from your stay in this body.

The soul, in contrast to the Higher Self, is the germ nature of your connection with Universal Oneness. The soul transcends mortal life. Even when you are stuck on the dharmic wheel and must constantly reincarnate because you have unfinished business (karma or sins you need to learn from), your soul can transcend space and time to always connect with the total and true infinite nature of life force. Your soul is connected to what Christians call the Holy Spirit, what Pagans call the nature of the Gods, what Buddhists call the Light of Buddha and what New Age believers call the Oneness of the Universal Spirit. It is your cellular blueprint on an energy level of true spiritual essence. Your soul is the guiding force to express, and *be,* love and enlightenment.

The intuitive part of your soul nature is called your "gut feelings." These are essentially your passionate soul nature in an unrefined form. If your gut feelings are love, joy, beauty and truth, then you can follow them fully and you will always be on your path. It is easy to be misled, however, if your passionate nature is controlled by fears, jealousies and material desires. To follow your soul nature, practice the skills in Appendixes A and B.

THE INNER AND OUTER SOUL

The outer expression of your soul connects with the wondrous infinite nature of all that exists. People usually have the profound ability to experience this only a few times in their life, if at all. These are the moments when you have a revelation that spiritually shifts you or makes you aware of the cosmic essence of oneness.

The inner expression of your soul is your passionate soul nature. This part of you expresses the needs and wants of your soul in this life—through your feelings, emotions, passionate nature and actions.

DO YOU RESIST YOUR BEAUTIFUL, SPIRITUAL NATURE?

The wonderful nature of your passionate soul propels you to love and live to your fullest. When you resist this beautiful nature because you must "do the proper thing," or you acquiesce to other people's concepts about right and wrong or good and bad, you are denying the active nature of your soul.

When you eventually leave this body, you have to answer to your higher nature or a higher power about how you accomplished your mission. What other people have said or done will not matter. What will matter is what you have said or done. Ultimately, you are responsible for your own actions. You are the person who must enact your soul mission throughout your life, using your own discretion and your own choices.

The more that you listen and act out of your soul nature, the more beautiful life becomes. Your soul gets lighter and brighter and expands to vibrate on the higher planes. If you connect with your soul nature, you become the essence of the living Buddha. To do this, you have to not only listen, but also act out of your soul nature. Buddha learned not to listen to other yogis and ascetics who told him that fasting and extreme methods of behavior would lead to enlightenment. He searched his own soul and discovered that the middle path was the best for him.

To walk your own path, you cannot imitate or conform to anyone else's. You will also have to push the ego of pride, arrogance and personal power aside, using simple meditation tools such as those presented in Appendixes A, B and C.

PASSIONATE SPIRITUALITY AND THE SOUL

People always ask, "How will I know when I am communicating with my soul nature?" When your soul nature is communicating with you, there is an immediate direct experience of being in touch with a profound feeling of oneness. You sense, know and feel that you are a part of the oneness and that whatever you are doing is right and true for you.

Your Higher Self might speak in a melodious or beautiful voice, but your soul speaks as if every cell in your body is vibrating with the right thing to do. It is an overall feeling as if all of you becomes aligned and automatically hears or feels your true essence. And yes, once you have been a part of this profound experience, you will always recognize it in the future.

Have you ever heard your soul speak to you? It can be like a whisper or a yell. It can be an image in your mind or just a simple knowing what to do. Your soul will speak to give you information or to get you to do the right thing on your true path in life. Communicating with the soul is often like watching a spiritual TV station. Souls speak through inner images you see in your mind's eye, or you may hear a voice that whispers, yells or sings. This is a grander and larger experience than just speaking with the Higher Self. It is as if you became one with all that there is. Often, people who have taken drugs receive a partial experience of their soul nature, but confuse this with a total experience. That is, drugs are impermanent, offering merely a slice of the true feeling of oneness.

An example of a partial feeling of oneness happens when you see a beautiful scene of nature, like a pristine grove of trees. But in a total feeling, you will also taste the trees, feel the trees, hear the trees, feel as if you are one of the trees and so on. In other words, all of your senses are engaged with what you are experiencing. On this higher level, your sixth sense allows you to KNOW and BE your experience as if you are truly one with it.

The ability to be in the oneness is a spiritual sense. For a moment, there is no separation between you and the experience. Your consciousness moves with the flow as if you are it, and also as if you are surfing it. When you experience this, it is your soul nature. However, when you get information and know things, but still have a sense of separation, this is from your Higher Self. In contrast, your soul nature is more profound, more moving and infinitely more connected to the oneness.

When you refuse to listen to your own information, when your emotional self is too willful or off-line, your soul will often "yell" at you or try to imitate a God nature. When this happens, people feel that they are hearing Jesus, a saint, a Bodhisattva, a god or goddess or a famous priest who is passing on communication. And yes, this is a very tricky thing to be clear about because sometimes we do communicate with these high spiritual beings.

Many times, though, it is just your soul talking with a megaphone, imitating this profound nature so you will listen. Most people do not know the difference and will automatically believe they have been contacted by the most high and holy. They will obey intently. But, spiritually advanced people know the difference between illusion and actuality. They have experienced soul nature a few times and recognize when their "God aspect" is the true voice speaking.

It is the job of your soul to keep you on-line so you accomplish your goals in this life, and it will do whatever it needs to do to accomplish this. It might seem a bit harsh, but it is actually the most important thing in your entire life. If you accomplish your mission, you can continue on in your next life to your goal. If you live your mission, your health is good, your energy is strong and you feel connected in every way.

When you are connected, you just know you are doing what is right and you feel good no matter what happens. When you are not connected, your life has more ups and downs, more traumas, as your higher nature keeps trying to twist and turn you, perhaps shifting your direction by ninety degrees or more to get you on your true path. Your soul nature mission is reflected in your true inner life, which you passionate soul expresses every day. Once connected, you will be able to stay balanced and happy.

Integrating your soul nature and passionate self

Have you ever felt driven to accomplish something? Have you felt so excited that you *had to* do something? Has anything overtaken your life and "forced" you to act it out?

When you are in touch with your true soul essence, it drives you to accomplish something in the outer world. Whether or not they verbally or intellectually understand the nature of their soul, successful people often feel they must do their obvious task in life. When you connect with your soul nature, every cell in your body turns on, tunes in and becomes one with your soul essence. Then you are automatically on your path, mirroring your soul essence and feeling the need to express your true passions.

Some people get in touch with their soul and then express their passionate nature. Others get in touch with their passionate nature, which leads them to communicate directly with their soul. Regardless of how you find the path to your ultimate soul essence, you must walk it for yourself. Integrating your soul nature and your passionate self is the ultimate act of living that opens the door to joy, love, accomplishment, health and your profound spiritual nature. Consciously or unconsciously, all human beings strive for this.

Shared visions of the soul

After World War II, the developed nations attempted to improve their industrial infrastructure, creating an economy to sustain them in peacetime. The focus of the nations moved from spiritual, philosophical and national interests to that of personal accumulation of goods and wealth within a competitive global economy. People looked increasingly to everything external: status items; designer products and goods; and building one's own financial base as a way to contribute to their country. The United States still leads as a global producer in this outward mentality, even though it has become enmeshed in a climate of war and conflict.

Nowadays, people are searching for moral and national values because they have somehow lost the meaning of life and of pride, both in themselves and their country. People in the States have pride in their burgeoning economy, but this is contingent upon having an economy that is always strong and constantly growing, and we all know that this may not always be the case. At the same time, many folks have all but lost touch with the meaning of life on all levels.

Slowly, but surely, however, we seem to be moving toward the creation of an ethic of personal integrity, which takes place on a higher level of vibration, wherein each person is to be held personally responsible for his or her own actions. This phenomenon of ethical integrity started after World War II, when soldiers were held responsible for following orders that were seen as crimes against humankind. Rape, pillage and genocide—crimes that in previous eras were acceptable actions of an invading army—were suddenly deemed to be personal, moral issues. Soldiers were informed that they should have exercised their moral judgment and not just followed orders from above that directed then to commit horrible acts against humankind. These new rules and values are now being tested throughout the modern world as we question our role, for example, in the war on terrorism.

The reasons and methodologies for group behavior, however, are not so strongly present. The world situation is forcing us to make individual moral decisions. On a clairvoyant, energetic and spiritual level, this is seen as the natural evolution of humanity—from persons who pledge allegiance to a specific country, to those who give higher allegiance to their soul nature. Once acting out of this higher soul nature," the individual is supposed to be evolved enough to act for the highest good of everyone on the planet. This growing soul integrity stems from individuals' God Source or God nature. Whether or not this will come to pass en masse is yet to be seen.

Shared visions of the soul come about when individuals have the power to act out of their own personal soul integrity, but also have the same collective vision. At present, many persons seem to be swinging back and forth from being controlled or influenced by negative group behavior, to being paralyzed by fear of defining their personal identity in a way that remains individual while also sharing the group process.

As a clairvoyant and spiritually defined Human Being, I strongly believe that many individuals are beginning to follow their own soul nature. If this happens en masse, we will have a consensus based not on cultural or national pride, but on higher dictates that will ultimately unite humanity. Such a direction will sustain us into the future and give meaning to our children. We, the human race, are a work in progress. I strongly suggest that you remember this when taking action in the world so that you represent the highest part of your soul nature and contribute your best.

CHAPTER 11
Integrating Your Passionate
Soul Into Daily Life

TO BE OR NOT TO BE

> "You don't get to choose how you're going to die, or when.
> You can only decide how you're going to live. Now."
> —- Joan Baez from "Daybreak"

There is a choice that you make when you incarnate in this body. You may think that this is about taking your life, but it is not. Your choice is whether or not you are going to embrace the life you have.

Many people view life as a strange and sometimes unwarranted gift given by their parents. However, the quality of living—of being alive enough to breathe, of loving and experiencing a multitude of tactile, mental and visual input—is only as good as what we give to ourselves. So even though we are given birth, we must establish the life force within us to experience the true gift of life.

We know that we are born into this life and that we die out of it. Some have even come to the realization that there is more trauma in being born, in entering this world on the physical plane of existence, than there is in dying. After all, it is only the people left behind who feel the pain of our leaving! Few realize, however, that once we are born, a mighty force of LIFE is in action. Once we get through the traumatic portal of birth, we can make our choice right away or spend years deciding. What is this choice? *To be or not to be*, to embrace the act of life wholeheartedly, full steam ahead, or to run from life at every turn.

To put it another way, some of us are born but never really bring our full focus here. Thus, we never truly begin the path of conscious action. Others move always toward death as if it were the final solution. Those who are more consciously evolved embrace the here and now, the I Am, the eternal present (past, present and future together). They have no problems, worries or guilt and they discover the secret of living by living in the present.

From the moment we are born, the force of nature breathes us alive. This invisible food for our bodies not only fills our lungs but also motivates every cell with energizing effects. We do not have to ask for breath. Programmed to breathe for us, our bodies can sleep, run in a race, climb a mountain or drive to work, and meanwhile we get just the perfect amount of air we need to help each cell do its job.

Another part of us, just as invisible as the air we breathe, also nurtures our body. It gives us a sense of purpose and all knowing, filling our minds with awe and peace. This invisible but potent part of us—our spirit—is holding out the thread of life for us.

All of us remember when we were so high-spirited that we seemed to be on top of the world. Or, perhaps we were so consumed by the present moment that there seemed nothing else in the world. The here and now was the most important event—everything. It could have been about cheering your friend on in a marathon race, going to a special event or concert, or simply falling in love. It is amazing how fully we live these timeless moments of action when there is no past, no future. It is even more amazing how infrequently we allow ourselves to experience special moments such as these.

Have you ever asked yourself why such cherished moments were so special? Perhaps it was because you were using *all* of you, infused with every ounce of your body and soul. But how often are we expected to BE here and be conscious? We usually don't even expect it of ourselves! Where are you right now? Are you here reading this page? Or is part of you getting ready to go somewhere, make dinner, call a friend or do a project at work? Remember that special time when everything rested on one moment of being? Maybe your consciousness wasn't divided and you weren't somewhere out ahead of yourself. Perhaps your passionate soul and your mind and body were acting in unison. If so, you were truly involved in the act of living.

Bringing all of your energy, your focus, your spirit, your mind and your body awareness into one place at one time is consciously making the decision to be alive. Actually, it is much more—this attention to the now can give you a mad passion for living. We have all seen "Night of the Living Dead" zombies walking on the street or maybe even been one of them for a period of time. These people have lost their spirit. They walk around programmed to get somewhere but do not enjoy themselves at all. They struggle through work and their problems, counting themselves lucky if they have a special moment. They have lost their ability to be *one* with their emotions, mind and spirit.

Once you decide to be alive, to make all moments special, it is really not so difficult to create this reality. After consciously deciding to take the plunge into life on every level, making it work is a piece of cake. Following the nature of your passionate soul, you are now on your true path in life.

Becoming conscious and aware

Your passionate soul is the emotional, "feeling" form of your self in action. It embodies the true nature of what you should do in this life. To integrate your true nature into your physical and mental experience, you need to become aware of your daily consciousness. In other words, to act out of your feelings, you have to know just what your feelings are. Consciousness is your ability to be aware of what you do, what you feel, what you think and how all this affects you.

Conscious awareness is a form of being sensitive to yourself, your environment and your experience of life. In this way, you can begin to discover just what your true internal motivations are in every situation. Once you understand why you do what you do, you can choose how to create the type of life you want to have. Understanding your actions and motivations enables you to understand and express your true passionate nature.

Do not fill yourself with too much TV, magazines, newspapers, music and entertainment. If you leave no time for contemplation, you will not pick up your inner messages. You will be too full of the evening news, the latest soap opera, the constant strains of your favorite band or singer and the newest hot movie star that delights you. You can do, or listen, or read or see all of these material things—but do not forget to leave room for *you*. You are an important person. You have feelings and thoughts, reactions and inner perceptions. To become more aware, try making some space to just see, notice, hear and allow.

Using your imagination

What you create in your mind and with your emotions is what you will experience. Take the time every morning to create your day. Visualize whom you want to meet, the types of experiences you want to have and what you would like to feel during the day. Clairvoyants often say that imagining something is seeing it in your mind's eye. When you see what you want on the movie screen of your inner perception, you are learning how to create it. You allow yourself to dream and then to make your dreams come true.

You can start by imagining your favorite food. Close your eyes and see your favorite food. Create it just the way you like it. Once you can create something simple like this, you can then go on to create such things as business deals, relationships, vacations and super great condos. You can create loving people in your life and wonderful experiences.

Everything "outside" of you is the creation of what you are inside. What you feel and think creates what you experience and do. If you can imagine the beauty and truth of your life, you can create it and thus liberate yourself with your own creation. In this way, you will release yourself from idle, negative and destructive thoughts. Your positive thoughts can then create beautiful actions.

Avoiding habituation

When you are a child, everything is new. Each experience is exciting and full of learning. When you are an adult, you become jaded in a way. You have already brushed your teeth thousands of times, strictly out of habit. Going to work and most other adult activities are also likely out of habit. When you are doing a thing by rote, you are simply doing it in your sleep. You are not consciously aware enough to evaluate what is happening, how you feel, or what you experiencing.

To become like a robot out of habit is to lose all feeling. You are not really living, you are just going through the motions. If you do this enough, you will begin to feel that life is boring. And it will be boring because instead of living, you will just be existing. People do this when they run errands or do things they feel they "have" to do. They get stuck on automatic.

On the way to work one morning, my neighbor got on the subway lost in thought. He told me later that out of habit he went to the office where used to work six months before being transferred across town. Why did he do that? Because he was not in his present consciousness. Being alive enough to enjoy the joys of living and the excitement of the moment means you have to constantly bring yourself into the now.

So, check in with yourself to see if you are living the moment or stuck in habit? What do you do by rote? What is new and exciting? What is so old that you don't enjoy it at all? If you find many things in your life are done by habit, see if you can change what you do, even slightly. Change it just enough to make life interesting or worth being "awake" for.

LISTENING TO YOUR MESSAGE

Once you are in the moment, you will recognize that you are getting messages. Life is full of messages that we often do not pick up. If you are in the moment, you will be able to "hear" your messages or "see" your messages or just "know" your messages.

When you hear your messages, your emotional soul is speaking internally through your inner voice. It is telling you what works and announcing what your powerful self wants and needs. It is your friend, your guide, your deepest emotion and your highest nature—all in one. It is, therefore, a good thing to listen to.

When you see your messages, you are being clairvoyant. The images in your mind's eye are like the TV of your mind. If you can see a food you like, a view of a loved one or the images in your dreams, you are practicing clairvoyance. It is my belief that everyone is clairvoyant. But, most people do not register that what they are seeing is an image in their mind. They just see it, accept it and do not question it as anything important. Seeing such a message helps you understand what you need to do. If you see the face of a loved one and feel you must call that person, for example, you are responding to your inner message.

Another way to receive a message is to be still and just know. If you meditate, you will notice that after twenty minutes or so you become very quiet within yourself. Many people receive information this way, although they may not know why or how the information comes. Knowing comes from your higher nature or your energy essence.

Everyone has this spiritual source, but not everyone makes use of the connection. Most people who consistently practice the meditation in Appendix C for three to five months start to receive messages from their higher nature.

RELEASING THE OLD TO CREATE THE NEW

To be a new you who enjoys life and follows your passions, let go of any old restrictions and allow new actions to take precedent. So, release your old way of doing things and create new patterns. Can you forgive everyone, including yourself? Once you do this, you can get what you want in life because you will not be hung up with the old. See Appendix A for forgiveness techniques, if you need them.

BANISHING YOUR FALSE PERSONALITY

Everyone has a false personality they may use at parties, in the office, with strangers, at public gatherings and even with relatives. But false personalities distance you from people, presenting an image that is a lie in your universe. This puts you out of touch with your feelings and your passionate soul. If you live a false personality, you are not acting out of your truth.

I went to a party at a friend's house the other day. I was amazed to watch my friend. I was amazed because the person I was seeing was not my friend at all but some strange character born on the pages of an etiquette book. My friend smiled graciously all of the time and made inane, small shallow conversation of the type she had often told me she despised. I asked her if she needed any help and she sweetly told me, "Thank you, but everything is under control." I knew she had been having a difficult time organizing this party thing and that she was under a lot of strain.

Being a close friend, I did not mind doing the behind the scenes party work to help her, and she knew that. And yet, when I asked her, I was publicly told that I was not needed, as if I were a stranger. I wondered what was really happening with her. When I got a chance, I wandered into her kitchen, the hot bed of organization for the hors d'oeuvres and drinks. This was where I would most likely discover the true story of what was going on. And sure enough, in this place where only the people hired to help were congregating, I found the true panic.

My friend walked in and did not notice me standing there. She was at the emotional point of pulling her hair out. Speaking to the person in charge of preparing the party trays, she vented her feelings.

"What will I ever do?" she asked no one in particular. "I don't know how to feed these wealthy people. There's no way I can make them feel at home."

It was then that I cornered my friend and asked her point blank just what was going on. She explained in tearful gasps that her husband, unbeknown to her, had invited his wealthy boss and she felt underdressed and ill prepared to host the party. Her husband was hoping to impress his boss, to get a better position that was currently up for grabs. My friend, however, felt she had not been given proper advance notice to dress properly and serve special food. She knew nothing of what was going on until these people had arrived on her doorstep.

Clearly, my friend was frazzled, her behavior erratic. From my viewpoint, she was trying to be someone she was not. She had erected what I call a false personality, creating a person she thought would please these wealthy, powerful people. But this was not *her* personality. When I had seen her in action at the party, I thought to myself that she was being cold and shallow. I had been shocked to see that in my friend. So now, I quickly sat her down and asked her what she wanted. Of course, she just wanted to impress them to help her husband.

I gave my friend some advice—you cannot impress people who are wealthier and more openly powerful in the world than you feel you are. But you can give them the gift of yourself.

I explained that she was a very warm, vibrant, loving person when she was her true self. This always showed through to the people around her, and that was why she had so many loving friends. This was her power in life. I said that she should be who she was instead of trying to imitate what she "thought" would make other people comfortable. I basically said, "Be yourself."

I told her not to compete with, not to try to impress, her guests but just to give them her natural warmth and the charm as she would offer any other visitors, whether they were friends, children, elders or family. She seemed to relax and realize how unbalanced she had felt when she was tying to be socially correct, instead of being herself.

Well, my friend listened to my advice. She went back into the party room and shared of herself the way she had always done at parties. She stopped worrying about what she was wearing and whether or not the food was "proper." She talked in her usual friendly manner, joked and listened to her unexpected guests as she normally did with everyone. I was overjoyed to see the real her emerge!

I didn't see my friend for a few weeks while I was away on business. When I returned, I called and asked about her husband's job and his boss. Her husband had won the coveted position, his boss making a point of how charming and warm his wife was. So her husband felt she had really helped him get the position. She thanked me profusely, saying that if she had behaved to please others the way she thought they wanted, she would have come across as a proper, but cold, hostess.

My friend learned that false personalities can distance people and hide the real you. She also started to value and respect her own worth. By being herself, she raised her self-esteem. She was not to be measured by her degree of wealth or social position or how she dressed. To value yourself based on your own internal worth is to regard yourself with unconditional love. So, love yourself not for what you do or how you appear in public, but for who you are right now. When you can accept yourself totally as you exist in the moment, the whole world loves you back. As a result, your life is filled with success, love, achievement and all other good things.

LOVING EVERYTHING AND EVERYONE

Most people are critical of things around them. It is easy to be critical in an imperfect world. But being negative does not make you feel good even though it might make you feel that you are better or special, because you want something superior to what exists. However, you may also become frustrated. It's not always easy to fix what exists right now.

You can practice finding out what you like about everything—and without having to be a perpetually happy-faced person. In reality, we all have our ups and downs. But, you can focus on the positive, on what pleases you about what you see and experience. This makes you feel happy, and your energy shines brighter.

Whenever you look at something—a person, an object, a situation, your job or relationship—make a list in your mind of what you like about it. Obviously, nothing is perfect, and there are many ways you could improve your life. If, however, you concentrate on the things you like and love about who you are and what is around you, soon it will be easy to make the changes you desire.

Always find what you like about a person or situation. If you like nothing, then get away from that person or situation because it is toxic to you. For the best in life, love your self and everyone and everything around you!

To love fully, often you will need to release your expectations of perfection. Use the skills of transforming energy in Appendix B to accept what is. If you are not obliged to live with perfect ideals, you may be surprised to find that you have allowed yourself to experience things more perfectly.

DEVELOPING YOUR VISION

If you really know what you want, you can get it. Not knowing what we want, most of us stumble around confused and disoriented. Right now is the time to decide what you truly want. It is time to get in touch with your passionate soul, your emotional body nature that represents your soul's desires in this body. It is the part of you that enacts your soul needs within your personal lifestyle.

To get in touch with what you want and then create an agenda to carry out your life vision, try following these steps:

1. Make a list of what you want and need in this life.

2. Next to each item, list what you will have to do to manifest this.

3. For each item, list your ego involvement on a scale of one to ten. One is the least involvement and ten is the most.

4. If your ego involvement for an item is above number 4, remove your ego involvement by placing the item in a box and blowing it up (see Appendix A) or by simply seeing it as flowing into the ocean and being absorbed. Do this energy technique ten times in a row, and then do it five times a day for two weeks until your ego involvement on your scale is number four or below. Ego tells us what we "should" do to be acceptable to our neighbors, or what makes us feel special, but it is not truly the connection with our passionate soul. As you release ego involvement, you get in touch with the true inner you that can create all your dreams in a neutral, loving manner. This benefits both you and those around you.

5. Now close your eyes and envision yourself as a person doing and having these things in your daily life. Does it work?

6. To reinforce your vision, record your guided vision into a tape recorder. Speak in the present tense of seeing yourself accomplishing these things in your daily life (e.g., I am …). When you feel overwhelmed or despondent about not creating your life the way you want it, take this tape and play back your positive affirmations.

TRULY ENJOYING WHAT IS

Whatever you have in your life right now is very special. It might not be all that you want, but it is what you have at the moment. It is important to validate how well you have created your present reality, thanking the powers that be (and yourself) for what is.

List everything you have in your life and be thankful for it. See if you can revel in the joy and wonderment of who you are. Sometimes, we seem to concentrate on what we do not have. This type of negative thinking makes you unhappy, as if what you have now is not as important! Once you can truly be joyous in the moment, it is easy to hook into the energy of your passionate soul nature and to create more of what you want.

For example, when I see someone who is obviously less fortunate than I am, instead of feeling sorry for or ignoring that person, I begin to thank the powers that be for my own life. Soon, I find that I do indeed have a great deal to be thankful for. Too often, in our materialistic society, we have been trained to emulate successful people who *seem* to have more than we do. This places us in a state of envy and disenchantment most of the time. Yes, a person who has more might be a role model if you are not experiencing jealousy. But, you also might be your own role model.

To create your own unique reality, you need to be in a constant state of love. This is to be like a child who has just discovered the wonderment of what he is and what he has. You can love yourself enough in each moment to create your next moment just as you like. So enjoy who you are and what you have right now.

FACING AND REMOVING YOUR FEARS

Basically, we are a matrix of love and fear. We never seem to get enough love, even when we have wonderful loving parents, and our fears seem to endlessly control us. To give yourself permission to access your passionate soul, you need to give yourself love and release your fears.

What do you fear? Most people have a lot of fears, but rarely will admit it. Here is a list of some of the most basic fears in life with which you might identify:

FEAR OF: losing my job or being fired or laid off.

FEAR OF: what other people think about me. Am I all right? Am I acting okay in front of other people? Do they like me? Am I dressed right for this occasion?

FEAR OF: being scolded by parents or the company boss or some person in authority.

FEAR OF: not being able to get into a particular school.

FEAR OF: not being able to get a particular job.

FEAR OF: not being accepted or being rejected.

FEAR OF: being alone.

FEAR OF: people not liking me.

FEAR OF: fear of natural disasters, such as earthquakes, fires and floods.

FEAR OF: unexpected crime.

FEAR OF: getting ill or dying.

Do not ignore your fears. Take your skill from Appendix B and use it to consistently release fear every time it comes into your consciousness. Release your fear, and it will not control you. We all have fears; this is normal. However, the more that you can train yourself to release your fear, the more you can direct your energy toward more positive things you want to create.

Do not dwell on your fears by spending time trying to understand them. Just use the skill in Appendix B to get rid of fear as soon as possible. As you release the energy of fear, it will return to you in a more neutral form. With greater clarity, you will find it easier to create your true-life desires. So, be brave and release your fears. Now you can freely choose what you want in life.

ENVISIONING YOURSELF AS HERO OR HEROINE

Try to envision yourself as your own hero or heroine. You are the person on a quest in life to find the answers, put the puzzle together, and discover the light at the end of the tunnel. It is always uplifting to find a great example of how another person handles a specific situation in life. It is certainly more empowering, though, to be your own hero or heroine.

Your passionate soul nature is your blueprint for your life's quest. Your actions are your agenda and your vision is your path. The end goal is being your best and doing what really empowers you. Empowerment is not just power but having the experience of love, joy, wonderment and the possession of life force in the body. Neither is empowerment just success in the worldly sense. Rather, empowerment is living your life to its fullest.

Clear yourself of all outworn concepts of empowerment using the skills in Appendix A and B, and then take the time to listen to your inner voice as it guides you on your quest toward real concepts of empowerment.

DISCOVERING YOUR LIFE'S PURPOSE

As you get in touch with your passionate soul, you will begin to discover your life purpose. I have often given personal session clairvoyant readings to help people access the agenda of their passionate soul. These readings do enlighten people and help them to gain focus. But, I have also noticed that most people already know their own agenda, even if on some unconscious level.

If you get rid of your fears, get in touch with your loving nature and allow yourself to connect with your passionate soul, you will intuitively begin to act out your life's purpose. You will be on the path of synchronicity. In other words, everything will just flow easily and happen naturally. All will come to you effortlessly, as it should.

PUTTING IT ALL TOGETHER

The law of diminishing returns states that, as you get older, if you do not find deeper and fuller sources of meaning in life, you turn off, tune out and lose touch with your emotions and your perceptions. There are several things that you need to do to keep yourself alive, awake and passionate about the act of living.

Your soul is always speaking and communicating with you. But, many people do not hear this until either the time is right or they have tired of hearing everything else. Then, suddenly they put the puzzle of their life together, and the visions of their soul become small yet powerful personal revelations. Take the time to clear yourself, to be still and listen to your personal revelations from your own inner voice.

Be true to yourself. Do what you *feel* is right no matter what other people say. This is your one chance at this life. Don't ruin your chance by living up to other people's standards or doing what other people would do. You are the best of who you can be right now. Yes, you will go on to do better, but you are a good person and you are doing your best.

For some people, life is a learning experience. For others, it is a test. In either case, release your hold on any negatives or fears and forgive everyone. Just experience the love of your soul. Love can help you move through all tests that life may hit you with. Then, everything that happens to you becomes a learning experience. If you are in touch with your passionate soul you will always do what is right for you.

If you believe in the ability to change yourself, then you will soon see how you can also change the world. I believe that when enough people become fully conscious, our world will rise out of the barbaric state in which we experience starvation, war and political repression. In this new world, people will interact harmoniously to create a peaceful, abundant life.

Once you have accessed your passionate soul, you will at some point come to realize that you are also connected to the soul of the entire planet. This awareness will help shift the entire global matrix toward a more positive alignment. As you personally shift, your very actions will bring beneficial changes in world around you. I know you will enjoy the world you are now learning how to create!

Appendix A
Skills to Realign Your Passionate Soul

To align your passionate soul with your life actions, you can learn certain simple, basic skills that bring your body, mind and spirit into balance. I would like to share some of the most useful clairvoyant skills here.

Why use these skills

Skills that you can use every day in any life situation are the easiest and best way to shift yourself when things seem not to work. Having energy skills is like being a carpenter and having a hammer, nails and a screwdriver. If you have the right tools, it is easy to get the job done. Hanging a picture or building some shelves without a hammer or a saw can be difficult indeed! Some of the tools here are basic for daily use, like the hammer and screwdriver of a carpenter. Other more powerful tools provide an easy way to accomplish something faster, like using an electric screwdriver instead of a manual one.

You can apply these skills consistently, integrating them into your daily lifestyle. Likewise, you will find that the skills help you know your inner self and thus integrate your true soul essence into your body. In this way, you will always be able to naturally express your passionate soul.

Grounding: Reconnecting with your body

Clairvoyants use the skill of Grounding to make a strong connection with the body. Grounding is an intuitive skill used in meditation, but it is also a very practical skill. It helps you to create your own reality, to bring your soul nature down to earth and to create a happy, healthy lifestyle that works for you.

First, find a chair with a straight back that you can sit in comfortably. Take off your shoes and make yourself comfortable. Close your eyes, take a deep breath and allow yourself to just relax.

Be aware of the base of your spine, and then imagine a ball of energy in this area. Now send some energy from the ball down through the chair, through the floor and through the ground all the way down to the very center of the earth. Hook the energy onto this center. For example, this stream of energy can be like a beam of light that goes down to and then encircles the center of the earth. Or it can be like a tree trunk with roots that go straight to the center of the earth and hook on. Or it could be like a chain with an anchor. Use whatever works for you. This is your grounding cord.

Having a grounding cord is like having a lightening rod on a house or an anchor on a ship. Grounding allows your body to feel safe and secure, as if you were anchored and supported by the whole earth. It also allows you to release any excess energy or excitement in your body. Now you can feel like you are here in present time, in the moment.

You can be grounded anywhere and everywhere you go. The grounding cord moves with you. It has a ball bearing that will turn toward the center of the earth when you lie down, or even if you stand on your head! Your grounding cord travels with you when you are in a car, a train, or a plane. It is your lifeline to the planet. On a symbolic and energy level, the whole planet is actually holding you up. This makes you feel naturally strong and secure in yourself.

When people first learn a skill, they usually try a bit too hard. This makes the skill more difficult to learn. It is best to use no effort at all and just *do* this. In the beginning, people may put a grounding cord down every twenty minutes or so—whenever they think about whether or not they are grounded. It takes about three months to get well grounded. Once you are really well grounded, you do not have to think about grounding. You just wake up in the morning, put your grounding cord down, and it will stay there throughout the day. If you lose your grounding, you will know it right away. For instance, you may start to go into confusion and not know what to do or how to get things done. When this happens, check your grounding; and if you have lost it, put down a new grounding cord.

CENTER OF YOUR HEAD: FINDING STRONG FOCUS

The Center of Your Head is an actual space that Mother Nature created so that you can keep your consciousness in the same place where your body is and develop your ability to focus. If you took x-rays of your head you could actually find this area. It does exist.

Getting into the Center of Your Head is a simple skill. It can be used for turning thought into action and for using active intelligence to get what you want in life.

First, take your fingers and place them at the top of your ears and point inwards. Draw an imaginary line across your head from one hand to the other—or from the top of one ear to the other. Now put one finger on your forehead, and place your other hand with the finger directly on the back of your head. Draw another imaginary line through your head. Where the two imaginary lines intersect is the actual center of your head.

Now, be *in* the center of your head. Yes, just take a deep breath, close your eyes and place your entire consciousness there. Take a good look around. Next, turn on all of the lights in this space, and look closely to see if anyone else is there with you. This should be an empty space, and it should belong to you and you alone!

Often you will find a friend, relative, parent, or child sitting in the center of your head. If you do find someone, say hello. But send the person back to his or her own body, because whoever is in this area is able to affect your body. If someone sits in the center of your head and thinks about eating, for example, your body will want to eat.

If you are looking at yourself sitting in the center of your head, or if you are looking *at* this center, then you are not sitting *in* the center. Make sure you are sitting directly in the center of your head and not viewing it like you would looking into the window of a shop.

Please do not confuse the center of your head with your mind! The analytical mind is a brain computer that enables you to process information and make rational judgments. The mind can analyze a situation and think. In contrast, the center of your head is a neutral space. Being there allows you to be focused, to be peaceful and still and to know what works for you.

Next, bring a large golden sun above your head, and let it come down into the center of your head. As it fills this space with radiant energy, own the center of your head and bring it into present time. Present time is being in the moment, in the here and now.

Although you are learning this skill with your eyes closed, you can use it all day long with your eyes open. You can ground yourself and be in the center of your head when you wake up in the morning. With practice, you will have more energy and wake up sooner and more easily. Soon you will find that you accomplish things more easily and that you get more done in a shorter period of time.

From the center of your head you do not have to think, listen, weigh, judge, consider or feel. When you are here, you can just be focused, peaceful, in charge and at one with yourself.

Blowing up boxes: Releasing the past

To get rid of your fears, you do not really have to face them, but you do need to recognize they are there. When you have a problem doing something, acknowledge that it is most likely because of reticence caused by some type of internal fear. If you do not know what this fear is, simply use the following skill called Blowing Up Boxes to release it.

I have updated this ancient skill for use in our fast-paced, modern life. It can be used with children as young as age six and adults as old as ninety. It works for everyone and will help you let go of sadness, grief, anger, resentment, fear and strong feelings. With strong emotions gone, it is possible to feel the joy, peace and wonderment of being alive in the moment.

Sit in a comfortable chair with your feet flat on the ground. Put down a Grounding Cord from the base of your spine to the center of the earth, and hook it on. Be in the Center of Your Head. Now create a big box about eight feet away. Use your imagination—your energy—to create this box. Put whatever you would like to let go of in the box. Do not look at it closely or examine it. Just put it in your box.

Now close up your box tight. Put a stick of dynamite under the box and blow it up. Blow up your box into tiny little particles of energy. Send everyone else's energy back to them (or wherever it came from) by just giving it a push or shove and telling it to go "home." Now bring your own energy back to you as a golden sun above your head, and let it come down and fill your body.

You can put anything in a box and blow it up. For example, you can blow up negative feelings, such as "I don't deserve this," "I'm not good enough," and "he or she doesn't like me." You can put a person into a box. It will not hurt that person. It will just release the person's hold on you. You can put a pain you have into a box. Sometimes you can release sixty to eighty percent of the pain immediately. Physical pain is a message from the body telling you that there is a problem. Once you recognize the situation and take action to fix it, you do not need to keep feeling the pain.

You can blow up boxes with your eyes open while you are walking down the street, riding on a train, working at your desk or conversing with someone. At first, practice this skill with your eyes closed so you will take the time to learn it well. Once you have practiced this way, you can blow things up in boxes all day long with your eyes open. Now you have an empowering vehicle that can change things for the better right when they are happening!

When you blow up something, make sure that *all* of it is in the box. Sometimes it is difficult to get every particle of it—your memories, feelings, emotions and so forth. This may happen if you are in resistance to letting go. Also, remember to send everyone else's energy back while reclaiming your own energy as a golden sun above your head that fills up your body.

You can blow anything up except for parts of your own body, because this can invalidate you. You can blow up pain, old feelings or fears and traumas and, if you blow them up enough, they will no longer affect you. The secret to using this skill is to use it constantly. After something unwelcome happens, immediately put it in a box and blow it up until the problem goes away.

BLOWING UP BOXES: RELEASING INVALIDATION

You may experience a natural drop in energy if someone invalidates you. Your self-esteem can diminish, and suddenly you do not believe in yourself as much. Not recognizing that they have been invalidated, some people begin to act out the invalidation by moving into negative or self-destructive behavior patterns. They may eat or smoke more, bite their nails, twitch their eyes, take prescription or illegal drugs, lose sleep; acquire nervous mannerisms, stop doing positive behaviors (such as exercise, healthy eating or hobbies) and sink into a depressed state of being.

Many times people do not know that they have invalidated someone. A friend who is jealous of your success, or a parent who has always wished to do what you are able to do, may invalidate you unconsciously. For example, the parent might verbally tell you how great it is that you are doing this thing, but an unconscious voice inside is saying, "I could not do this, so you will probably not be able to do it either."

These are normal human reactions. You may be invalidated because you look different, are of a different race, come from a different city or culture, have an accent, have different beliefs or values and so on. When others invalidate you, it makes you feel down, depressed and a little out of touch with your passionate self.

If someone has unconsciously invalidated you, then take what you think is the invalidation and put it in a box and blow it up. Do this at least twenty times or until you feel better. Clairvoyants see invalidation as a dark blue energy, but not everyone "sees" energy or colors. You do not have to see invalidation to get rid of it. It is easier if you do feel that the invalidation is there. But you can just suppose or postulate that someone has invalidated you. Take that energy from your body or your energy field (your aura), or your general consciousness, and simply put it in a box. Now blow it up, and it will get released. The other person's energy will return to him, and you will feel your normal, happy, balanced, positive self once again!

BLOWING UP BOXES: DISCOVERING JOY IN THE MOMENT

Most people live in the past, or yearn for and live in the future. The key to getting in touch with your passionate soul is to live in the moment. Bring your consciousness, your feelings, your mind and your body into present time. Just envision that you are right here, right now. If there is anything you are thinking or feeling that takes you out of the present moment, put it in a box and blow it up.

Enjoying life is not just a state of mind; it is an action of the moment. Instant happiness is the ability to like yourself for who you are right now. This is who you are at the present, and—good, bad, or indifferent—you are the best of who you are at this moment. Present time is a powerful concept that can work for you. It allows you to enjoy who you are right now and to connect with the inner feelings of your passionate soul.

Present time is being able to bring all of your thoughts, actions and energy—*all of you*—into the here and now. When you are in the present moment you do not have problems. You have solutions. Yes, you almost automatically find your solutions. When you are in the present moment you do not agonize over the past or worry about the future, because you just listen as your passionate soul takes action in the moment.

Sit down in a comfortable chair. Put your feet flat on the ground. Put a Grounding Cord down from the base of your spine to the center of the earth and hook it on. Be in the Center of Your Head. Now close your eyes, take a deep breath and say hello to yourself. Let all of the tension in your body flow down your grounding cord. Relax and be right here in the moment. If there is anything that stops you from being in the moment, just put it into a box and blow it up. If there is anything that stops you from feeling good about yourself, loving yourself, or enjoying this present moment, put it into a box and blow it up. Blow up whatever you are thinking about and just allow yourself to be in the consciousness of the now—this very moment in present time.

Bring all of yourself into present time:

Bring your feet into present time. Just conceptualize that your feet are in present time—right here, right now, in the moment.

Bring your legs into present time. Right here, right now, in the moment.

Bring your abdomen into present time.

Bring your hips into present time.

Bring your solar plexus into present time. Right here, right now, in the moment.

Bring your chest into present time.

Bring your lungs and your heart into present time.

Bring your shoulders into present time. Traditionally, shoulders are the spot where we carry our burdens, so if you have a lot of responsibilities right now, put them into a box and blow them up. Now, bring your shoulders into the present moment, in the here and now.

Bring your arms into present time.

Bring your throat and neck into present time.

Bring your head into present time.

Bring the center of your head into present time.

Bring your mind into present time. Right now, in the moment.

Bring your whole body into present time, right here, right now, in the moment.

CREATE A GAUGE: GETTING INFORMATION

There is a simple clairvoyant skill that you can use to get information about yourself. First, sit down and ground yourself, close your eyes, put all of your consciousness and energy in the center of your head, and take a nice deep breath. Blow up anything that is on your mind so that you are in a good clear space. Bring yourself into Present time.

Now, Create a Gauge that is like a thermometer. It goes from zero to one hundred percent. Put some bright red energy in your gauge. When you want to know something simple ask the question and look at your gauge. An example is asking yourself how much you really want to do a particular job. Now look at your gauge, and the first percentage number you see is almost always what it is.

This is a simple method for getting your basic answers in life. If you find yourself thinking or wondering too much, simply blow up your "mind" thoughts in a box. Then go back to looking at your gauge. When you are finished looking at your gauge, put it in a box and blow it up.

Make a list: Getting to know yourself

You are your own best resource in life. If you truly know what you want, you can get it. But, often we get confused and try to get what our neighbors want, what a friend desires, or what the latest new status item seems to be. During one year, every person who came to me for career counseling had read a certain magazine article describing the newest career choices. They all wanted to change careers to become one of the top moneymakers like those listed in the article. Unfortunately, the careers did not suit many of the people I talked to. It is wise to get to know yourself, what you want most and what you do best. There is truth, and it is always inside of you.

Learn to make lists. Make a list of all of your skills and abilities with a percentage choice of how much you like to do this particular skill. (Percentage is how much you would like to do this all day long.) For instance, would you like to cook ten percent of your day or eighty percent of your day? If this your life's desire, you would probably cook one hundred percent of the time if you could.

The following is a list I made for myself:

Skill	Percentage of Time I Like To Do This
Writing	80% (I really do enjoy writing)

136

Teaching   100%   (I do this all day long and really enjoy it)

Cooking   10%   (I am a good cook but would not do this all day!)

Graphic Arts Paste-up 20%   (I am good at graphic arts but would not choose to do it a lot)

Bookkeeping 01%   (I am not good at this and hate doing it.)

Racquetball 10%   (I like to do this but only about once a week)

Walking   80%   (I love to walk)

Filing   08%   (Mostly I hate to do this but sometimes find it interesting)

Make lists about yourself until you begin to get to know yourself well. Make lists of what you do and do not like, and why. You are your own best resource if you know your skills, your good and bad points, your desires and your fears.

Make lists of skills you would like to learn. Make lists of hobbies that you enjoy. Make a list of all of your life dreams. Make a list of your fears and then use the skills presented here to release them one by one.

Take action: Release your fears, one by one, over a period of the next three months or more. Using your list, pick your best occupation, a hobby that will most fulfill your passionate desires and the general activities you can be doing to express your passionate soul nature. Show you what you really want to do, not what you think you "should" do. By viewing your lists, you can switch to actions that reflect the true you.

Telling the truth from the lie

We all tell social lies to the people around us. It may start with the simple daily question of someone asking how you feel. Most people are trained to always answer "fine" or "okay." The proper answer is always "I'm having a great day," right? It does not matter if you were just in an accident, or lost your job or got sick with the flu.

It is all right to respond in the traditional, wonderful way as dictated by our social culture, but it is also very important to know *inside* what the real truth is. That is, always tell the truth to yourself. Sometimes, when people tell a lot of social lies, they get out of touch with the real truth inside. Here is a small skill for knowing the truth from the lie. Use it when you want to know if someone else is telling the truth.

Create two boxes. Put the concept of Truth in one box and the concept of Lie in the other. Now, take a tiny pinch of the person's energy you want to know about, and put it in both boxes. The box that represents your answer will light up brightly. You can also do this: Creating your two boxes and simply ask the person's Spiritual Being to light up the one that is truly representative. Both of these techniques take a little time to master, but once you get them to work, they will always tell you the truth.

Create a gauge: Permission

Many people know what their passionate soul wants to do, but they listen instead to friends and relatives who advise the "proper" or "right" thing. It is important to have your own permission to do only what is right for yourself. If you do not follow the passion of your true soul nature, you may have karma that carries over to your next life. You may also create a misalignment of emotions in this life, which can cause poor health, confusion, negative self-esteem and lack of true focus.

Use a gauge to give yourself permission for what you most want to do. Take your gauge, put some bright red energy in it, and ask how much permission you have:

To love yourself?

To enjoy yourself right now?

To express your true passionate soul?

To have the career of your choice?

Ask yourself all of the questions about who you are and what you want to do. If your permission is very low, raise it up five percent each time you look. If you raise your permission level five percent every other day, you will soon have higher permission. If you raise it up all at once, usually it will just sink back. Try to raise up your permission consistently over time so it gradually becomes acceptable to you.

COMMUNICATING WITH YOUR PASSIONATE SELF

Close your eyes. Blow up whatever you are thinking or feeling right now, until you are completely right here and now in the moment. Now envision yourself in your favorite vacation spot. (Fill in your favorite spot. I will use a beach here for an example.)

Hear the ocean, feel the sand under your feet and the warm sun on your body. Watch the palm trees blow in the wind and listen to the marvelous sounds of the waves hitting the beach. Here you are—you and your passionate self.

Talk to your passionate self as if it is a good friend who is here with you. Ask what it really wants that would make it feel good right now. Once your passionate self tells you, decide if it is possible for you to do this within the next month. If it is possible, thank your passionate self and promise you will do this within the next month. If you feel that this is impossible to do at the moment, then tell that to your passionate self. Ask it for some other thing that it wants in life. When you finish, bring yourself back to your body, to the current reality.

Is it your passionate soul or an obsession?

An obsession controls you so that you feel you have to do it no matter what. You feel you *must* follow your obsession to feel good. When you are obsessed, you feel out of control, as if a force larger than you is *forcing* you to behave in this fashion.

When you are acting out of your passionate self, you feel as if your whole world has just come into balance. Following your passionate soul fulfills your need to be your true essence on earth, and so you will have a feeling of completeness and oneness. Everything begins to make sense—this feels right and whole. You are instantly grounded and in touch with all levels of your universal self. People who have had sudden revelations in meditation also recognize this experience, which is the basically the same physical reality as instant personality enlightenment.

Guided meditation to your passionate self

With a tape recorder or mini tape deck, record this guided meditation in your own voice. Then sit back, close your eyes and go on a guided meditation to visit your passionate self:

Take a nice deep breath. Bring yourself into the moment, into right here and right now. If there is anything that stops you from being here right now, put it in a box and blow it up. Blow up all problems and mind chatter that is going on right now. Bring yourself into a quiet still place.

Now create a "magic" magic marker and draw a doorway to the astral, or energy, plane. Open your doorway and step through it into a beautiful grassy plain. Close the door behind you, but remember where it is located.

Right in front of you there is a large, impressive stone throne that forms a chair fit for a king or a queen. Walk to the stone chair and sit in it. You can hear the crickets in the grass and feel a warm wind on your face; the strong sun on your head and the warmth left in the stone now fills your body.

You are the king or queen of your life. As you sit on this throne, allow yourself to be in charge of your kingdom and to create your life the way you want it to be. Envision yourself as a beautiful being, and see your body in the strength and healthy youth of the moment. Whatever you create while you are on the energy plane will happen for you. So ask your passionate self what it *really* wants and then, as your own king or queen, make it so!

Envision yourself having, being, or doing the actions that truly please your passionate soul. Whatever you imagine will have some reality in your future in your true life. After you have finished "seeing" the future as you want it to be, stand up and walk back to your astral doorway, open it and step through it right back into your body. Put your feet into your feet, your hands into your hands, your head into your head, face forward and take a nice big deep breath. You are now back in present time in the moment.

FINDING THE "I AM" STATE OF AWARENESS

Being in the I Am awareness of the present moment is being the most alive that you can be at this time. It is being clear enough to accept yourself in a peaceful Buddhic state that says there is no judgment, no fault and nothing to live up to but the very state of existence. You are perfect just the way you are, in touch with the oneness of the universal life force. You are just being with the true unconditional love that allows you to exist without justification.

To be the I Am state of awareness is to experience one special moment of enlightenment. There is no fear, no anxiety, no performance, no needs—*just being who you are in the moment.*

There are many things you can do to reach this state. The skills of Grounding, Center of the Head, Releasing Emotions and Running Energy that are presented in Appendix A and B will get you to this awareness over a period of time. Some people take a few months and some people need a few years, but if you practice these skills consistently, you will get to the I Am state.

You can also reach the I Am state of awareness by simply releasing all of your responsibilities, fears, anxieties and desires and forgiving yourself for not being perfect. Some people experience this state when they allow themselves to become totally absorbed in a creative project, an athletic experience or anything that entirely absorbs them at the moment.

Releasing programs

All of us have programs that tell us what to do. Many are our own programs, but some were given to us by other people to control us or to enforce a sense of morality within us. However, you do not need a program to live your life well. To release all programs, simply take your feeling or concept of these, put them in a box and blow it up.

To recognize a program, be aware of when you repeat orders to yourself, or you do something because you think or feel that you "have to," or because "everyone else" does that, too. Programs are separate and apart from the present moment, in which you can make your own decisions rather than having a program make the decision for you. Whenever you feel that the decision has already been made, it is a program. To truly have free will and the ability to make your decisions in the moment, you need to blow up all of your programs.

Some programs are moral programs that tell you what is right and what is wrong. Children might require this instruction, but evolved spiritual Beings (as we are becoming) need to make decisions from their higher spiritual nature. The easiest way to exercise free will and release these programs is to blow them up. You have to do this a lot until the energy dissipates. You can also see the program as melting into the ocean and returning to its source.

PUTTING IT ALL TOGETHER

If you follow the exercises of Grounding, staying in the Center of Your Head and Blowing Up what is not wanted in your life, you will feel clearer and more focused. As confusion and fuzziness disappear, you will be more in touch. Staying in present time enables you to release fears, worries and problems, always accessing the best solutions for your life. Using your gauge, you can figure out how much you really want to do things, getting in touch with your true inner information. Making lists is the way to know yourself intimately and to do what really works for you.

Each of these life skills is useful and interesting on its own, but put together the whole becomes a dynamic, workable life system. On this path, you can forever stay in touch with your passionate self as the ideal lower-body expression of your soul. That is, once you are really in touch, you are acting from your highest nature on the most physical level. Giving yourself permission to do this is giving the true gift of free will and spiritual enlightenment in daily living.

Appendix B
How to Shift Fast

When we get stuck or slow down in our growth, we may go into confusion. We may feel either that life has either passed us by or that what we want just will not work. It is important to keep developing, to keep shifting and changing. As a result, your Being gets the message that you are accomplishing something and going in the direction of your choice. Here are ways you can shift fast:

1. Give yourself permission to love yourself for who you are right now. Once you love yourself, you can give more to yourself and grow faster. Often we unconsciously love ourselves only *after* we accomplish something. Next time, first love yourself unconditionally, and then everything will work more easily!

2. Forgiveness is often a key to releasing old emotions. This can seem difficult, but simply allow yourself to forgive everyone in your life. If your Being seems to resist, put this resistance in a box and blow it up until all your resistance disappears. Forgiveness allows you to release hurt and to move into present time.

3. Create a guided visualization in which you see yourself doing what you want to do. This is similar to what Olympic athletes do the night before the big day! They close their eyes and visualize themselves running the race perfectly and winning. Visualize yourself rewriting the script of life to be what you want it to be. When the unconscious mind creates the future in this way, the conscious self somehow hears it internally and tries to make it come true!

4. Let go of your perfectionist self. This planet is not a perfect place. Give yourself permission to change and shift, to grow and accomplish even though you are not perfect. Perfection is an ideal. You can accomplish your dreams even when you are not perfect. Put your perfect ideals in a box and blow them up over and over again.

5. Create a humorous situation. Make yourself the heroine or hero of your own cartoon strip and regularly laugh at yourself. The more humor you have about yourself and your life, the more quickly you will shift.

6. Praise yourself continuously for everything you have and everything you do. Treat yourself with respect and praise. You are the best of who you can be right now. Yes, you will go on to get better and better, but treating yourself well allows you to change faster. If you do not believe this, just view how children change. If you praise children they try harder; if you scold them, they shrink in on themselves and hide from view and hurt. Praise yourself so you will feel good enough always to follow your passionate soul's path.

7. Speak to your passionate soul every day. Feel your passionate soul every day. Often say yes to yourself, giving permission to act from your core. When you were a child, your parents protected you by saying no—"Don't cross the street, don't touch

the hot stove. Their nos were usually much more frequent than their yeses. So, say yes to yourself now.

Celebrate your life

Every day, list five things describing what a great person you are. Take the time to know and trust yourself and your decisions. Celebrate your big decisions in life by treating yourself to something special. It might be a special cup of tea, a dessert or a little gift for yourself.

Practice the "I Am" state in the present moment as a soul Being. Say to yourself, I am aware of the wind on my face, the sun on my head, the humidity and the water in the air, the smell of the plants, the sounds around me and so on. I am just what I experience in the moment, and I am connected to the universe. See, feel, smell, hear, sense and know the "I Am" within you. Close your eyes and breathe in the entire universe as a living entity that surrounds you, but is also within you.

Create five of your favorite positive inner statements (positive reinforcements), and say them whenever you feel any type of insecurity. If you tend to forget these, then write them down in short form on a piece of paper. Attach this to your books, your key chain or items you use regularly. When you see them, remember to repeat them subvocally on an internal level.

Make a list of your passionate soul desires, and strive to accomplish these every day in every way.

Releasing conflict now

Everyone has some kind of inner conflict. Learn to recognize and release conflict in the moment. Unfinished business with someone or unresolved emotions, such as guilt or fear, will produce inner conflict.

Envision yourself standing on the beach. Visualize that all the conflict within you flows out of your body, down into the earth and then into the sea. Your conflict just runs out of you into the ocean, where it is absorbed and released. Fill the part of you that released the conflict with cosmic love energy that is the color of pink, peach or rose.

Whenever you have conflict, allow it to run out of you and down to the ocean. Do not experience the conflict! Just send it, like a giant stream of energy, to be absorbed by the ocean.

HUGGING A TREE: FILLING YOUR ENERGY SELF WITH LIFE FORCE

If you release energy and feel a loss, or if you just feel out of touch or lacking within yourself, you can boost your energy simply by Hugging a Tree. If you cannot find a tree to hug, then close your eyes, envision a tree and imagine that you are hugging it.

Or, find a tree to look at, then close your eyes and see and feel yourself hugging it. Trees will take your pain and sadness, your sorrow and loss and will give you back energy. Trees with pine needles are known to give you the most energy.

FINDING YOUR LIGHT SELF

Speak to God. If you are Christian, speak to Jesus. If you are Buddhist, speak to Buddha. If you are Shinto, speak to the Gods. If you are Muslim, speak to Allah. If you are Pagan, speak to the god and goddess of your choice.

When you speak to God, ask for the gift of light to fill you. Usually, you have to give a gift of yourself back to God. So offer something, perhaps what you are willing to do. Many people offer their love. For example, they will give love to a friend or do something for the environment, such as planting a tree, cleaning their block, caring for an animal, doing a good deed or giving to a charity. The more personal your offering, the more you might be listened to. The gift of light you receive in return lets you see within yourself. You will feel enlightened to always be on your path as a soul Being. When you have this light within, it is easy to reach out and express yourself through your passionate soul.

Are you the child, adult or parent?

Which one of these roles do you play the most often and with whom? Create a thermometer-type gauge that goes from zero to one hundred percent, and put some bright red energy in it. Ask yourself the following questions, and watch for the very first answer you receive:

How much, during an average day, are you the Child? The Adult? The Parent?

How much of your behavior is the child when you are with your parents? When you are with your Boss? When you are with your friends?

When are you the Adult? When are you the Parent?

Why are you the Child? Why are you the Adult? Why are you the Parent?

Which is easiest for you to be? What makes you feel the most comfortable? Why?

If you want to shift any of this, then blow up the behavior you want to change. Blow it up while it is happening. Blow it up afterwards. And blow it up now while you are thinking about it.

Running energy:
Meditation for soul alignment

The Clearsight method of Running Energy instantly and automatically aligns your Higher Self and your soul nature with your body personality in this life. If you practice this meditation for at least twenty minutes every day, you will feel a shift within one month. This meditation relaxes your body, cleans your energy centers (chakras), clears your aura (your life force energy) and purifies every cell. Running energy allows an instant soul connection as it cleans and clears old and unnecessary energy debris from your space. Now you can access your true personal universe.

You can easily change the quality of your life just by practicing this new type of meditation every day. Running energy is like taking an energy shower, washing away outworn patterns and other people's energy, concepts and ideas from your own body's system. *Now you are able to use your own free will to feel secure and relaxed in making your own choices.*

How to run energy: At the bottom of your feet are energy centers that open and close like the lens of a camera or the iris of an eye. Be aware of these centers and open them up to a place that seems comfortable for you. Then, conceptualize bringing up about fifteen percent earth energy through your feet, up your legs, through your thighs, up to the base of your spine and down your grounding cord. Now keep that energy running. You are bringing fifteen percent earth energy up your feet and up your legs, all the way up to your tailbone and down your grounding cord.

You can visualize earth energy as being whatever color is comfortable for you—many people use green or brown. If you tell yourself to bring up fifteen percent earth energy, you will get this. If you tell yourself you want fourteen or sixteen percent, you will get whatever you ask for. Your internal energy self can measure exactly! Please do not use more than fifteen percent. This earth energy will give you solidity and strength, yet enable you to release tension in your legs.

At the top of your head is an energy center that looks like a crown. It also opens and closes like the iris of an eye or the lens of a camera. Be aware of the energy center at the top of your head (while holding your consciousness in the center of your head), and open your crown center. Imagine it opening up as a spiral to a place that is comfortable, and allow about eighty-five percent soft golden cosmic energy to come down your crown center, along the back of your spine and into the base of your spine, where it mixes with the earth energy coming up your legs.

As they merge, the two energies have a natural mixing action and form a pumping movement, which propels the energy up the front of your spine and out your head. Some of the energy branches off and moves across your shoulders, down your arms and out the palms of your hands. Some of the energy also goes back down your legs and out your feet. Let any excess energy go down your grounding cord. Now keep this energy constantly running.

Run energy for five or ten minutes at a time in the beginning. When you wish to stop running energy, bend over and stretch, drop your head and arms toward the ground and let any excess energy that has collected on top of your head or on your shoulders run out into the ground. This easy process is called Dumping Energy.

Now, sit up in the chair, open your eyes, take a good look around and get your bearings. Running energy often places you in an altered state of consciousness, so you may want to take another moment to bring yourself back to "normal." Notice that your entire system may be in a state of relaxation and calmness, putting you in touch with your own awareness and the oneness of the universe. As you learn this meditation, you may also notice that many things in life seem simpler and easier to accomplish.

You can do this daily meditation for at the beginning or end of the day, or just sit and run energy during the day to feel less tense. When you are finished, please remember to always let go of any extra energy as you bend over, stretch and drop your head and arms toward the ground. If the energy sits on your head or your shoulders, this might cause a headache or feelings of sluggishness. Often people who sit at their desks for long periods of time get headaches or stiff shoulders from the excess energy that collects, unless they bend over and let it flow to the ground.

While you run energy, close your eyes and sit in a chair with your feet flat on the ground so the energy will run through your legs. Running energy does not work if you are sitting on the ground with your legs curled up in a lotus position. Your legs are your action machine. You think something, and then your legs move to take action. If you are out in the countryside, use a big rock or log to sit up on. If you have an apartment or home where there are no chairs, buy a small portable picnic chair to sit on.

Always consciously complete your meditation by dumping energy. Some people think a lot while running energy. If any of your thoughts or feelings stop you from experiencing relaxation or peacefulness after running energy, then put them in a box and blow them up.

The running energy meditation combines cosmic and earth energies. As these neutral energies flow through your body, you will naturally allow yourself to relax and be calm while still feeling energized. As you become at one with your true essence, you will be more enlightened about yourself and your purpose in living.

Appendix C
Suggested Reading List

Remember Your Essence by Paul Williams

1987, New York: Harmony Books

ISBN 0-517-56524-2

The Fourth Way by P.D. Ouspensky

1971, New York: Vintage Books

ISBN 0-394-71672-8

The Ecstatic Journey by Sophy Burnham

1997, New York: Ballantine

ISBN 0-345-039507-7

The Five Stages of the Soul by Harry R Moody and David Carroll

1997, New York: Anchor Books

ISBN 0-385-48225-6

The Body of Light by John Mann and Lar Short

1993, New York: Tuttle

ISBN 0-8048 19920

The Angels Within Us by John Randolph Price

1993, New York: Fawcett Columbine

ISBN 0-449-0784-8

Mental Fitness by Michiko J. Rolek

1996, New York: Weatherhill

ISBN 0-8348-0373-9

God and Man by Masahisa Goi, translated by Shunsuke Takagi

1983, Chiba, Japan: Byakko Press ISBN –89214-065-1

White Light Association 5-26-27, Naka-Kokubun, Ichikawa, Chiba,

Japan Postal District 272.

About the Author

Levanah Shell Bdolak, the author of this book has been leading seminars in consciousness transformation skills since 1972 and travels nationally and internationally showing people how to shift their consciousness in easy practical ways. She shares these and other skills with executives and housewives in Tokyo every month at the Clearsight Japan Center and has taught internationally in Japan, France, Hong Kong, Thailand, Great Britain and nationally throughout the United States. She has shared these skills with nurses, doctors, physicists, therapists, artists, executives, chefs, entertainers and housewives. Levanah is a professional Clairvoyant, a motivational speaker, and a founder of the Clearsight Center in Santa Monica, CA, existing since April of 1980, where seminars are offered in a wide variety of subjects.

www.ingramcontent.com/pod-product-compliance
Lightning Source LLC
Chambersburg PA
CBHW061250280526
45784CB00002B/704